THE RETURN

TRUMP'S BIG 2024 COMEBACK

DICK MORRIS

Humanix Books
www.humanixbooks.com

Humanix Books

THE RETURN by Dick Morris

Copyright © 2022 by Humanix Books

All rights reserved.

Humanix Books, P.O. Box 20989, West Palm Beach, FL 33416, USA

www.humanixbooks.com | info@humanixbooks.com

Humanix Books is a division of Humanix Publishing, LLC. Its trademark, consisting of the words "Humanix Books," is registered in the United States Patent and Trademark Office and in other countries.

ISBN: 9-781-63006-207-1 (Hardcover)

ISBN: 9-781-63006-208-8 (E-book)

Printed in the United States of America

10 9 8 7 6 5 4 3 2 1

To Eileen

Contents

PART III
The Message: Democrats Have Made
America Unrecognizable

Author's Note

As I write this book, I feel like I am doing so with only one hand. It is the first book in twenty years that I have written without my co-author, lover, best friend, muse, goad, inspiration, role model, coach, attorney, political advisor, motivator, perfectionist, cheerleader, and wife of forty-four years by my side. Writing without her is like hearing one hand clapping.

But she'll be back.

Eileen McGann was felled by a stroke on March 29, 2021. To quote FDR, it is a date that will live in infamy.

Thanks to the Lord and hundreds of prayers, she never lost her ability to speak with all her usual style, grace, perspective, and dry wit. Walking is more of a challenge, but she's getting there.

Once, Steve Doocy, on *Fox and Friends*, asked me what it was like writing with my wife. I explained: "A lot of people assume that she does the research, and I do the writing. But that's not how it works. We divide the book in half, and she writes half, and I write half."

Then Steve asked if she ever says, "Honey, I love you, but this isn't much good."

"Well, Steve," I replied, "she usually skips the first part."

We have written twenty books together, including thirteen *New York Times* bestsellers. God, how I miss her.

Well, here goes!

—*Dick Morris*

Introduction

ALL IS NOT LOST. Thank God we live in a democracy with regular elections, and what liberty and democracy have lost in one cycle can be restored in the next.

It's our last chance!

In past elections, we were always told that the stakes have never been higher. Pundits regularly warn us about the consequences of the other party winning. The other party will bring disaster. But the elections of 2022 and 2024 are different. The other party already won the election of 2020—sort of—and disaster is already upon us.

To win these next two elections, we must realize that there are new rules under which any electoral battle in the future will now be conducted. We must adjust to them and learn to win under them.

But before we turn ahead to the coming contests, let's frankly and honestly answer the core question:

Did Donald Trump win or lose the election of 2020?

Would a fair vote count of only timely ballots cast by eligible voters award the election to Trump or to Biden?

The deliberate efforts of the Democratic machine politicians in swing states to conceal and obfuscate the truth has meant that we may never know the correct answers to either question. And the cowardice of the US Supreme Court provides us no help or clarification.

Filling this critical information gap are the various state-sponsored audits of the 2020 election, now under way in Arizona, Georgia, and Wisconsin. We hope that they will give us an accurate portrait of what happened in the 2020 election.

But one thing is clear: The voter turnout, on both sides, was overwhelming, vastly outpacing any in modern history. The turnout in 2020 exceeded that in 2016, just four years earlier, by almost 20 percent

Americans reversed almost a century of low voter turnout.

It's a whole new country that voted in 2020. From 2000 to 2020, voter turnout rose by 51 percent, while voting age population went up by only 21 percent.

Everything we knew—or thought we knew—about American politics is obsolete in this new era of massively higher turnout.

Did the Democrats win because of fraud? Was the election stolen?

It's certainly true that many paper ballots were forged or cast in the names of voters who had died or moved away—or who simply did not exist. The absence of photo ID—because Democrats refused to require, or even permit it—guaranteed that. Particularly with ballots cast via drop boxes and serviced by Democratic Party workers, many Trump ballots doubtless were never tallied.

Much of the fraud involved real, active voters casting real ballots but doing so after the time deadlines specified by law.

Still, more were cast by eligible voters under the in-person pressure of a Democratic election worker standing in the doorway, compromising their right to a secret ballot.

We can and must change these laws and administrative procedures to stop post-election voting, drop boxes serviced by party workers, and ballot harvesting. We've got to require full signature verification, and above all, we must require photo identification to register and vote. We must demand that every mail-in ballot has the last four digits of the Social Security number correctly entered.

However, the likelihood is that, even had we done all that, we probably would still have lost the national popular vote. The Republican fortunes might have been rescued by carrying certain swing states to provide an electoral majority, even amid a popular win for the Democrats.

Were the elections in Arizona, Michigan, Wisconsin, Pennsylvania, and Georgia free from Democratic shenanigans, Trump probably would have won some, or all, of these states, likely enough to carry the Electoral College and re-elect him president.

But we must not let this likely fact obscure the equally evident reality that more people voted for Biden than for Trump, by a massive number. How often can we expect the geographic distribution of the vote to rescue us from oblivion?

It is the essential premise of this book that we must examine why we lost the popular vote by such a margin, and focus on winning it in the future. We cannot, and should not, expect to stay in power by frustrating the will of the majority of the voters just because the Constitution says we can. Majority rule is still the bedrock principle of democracy.

Out of fifty-eight presidential elections, the popular vote winner lost in the Electoral College only five times: in 1824 (John Quincy Adams's defeat of Andrew Jackson), 1876 (Rutherford B. Hayes's defeat of Samuel Tilden), 1884 (Benjamin Harrison's victory over Grover Cleveland), 2000 (Bush over Gore), and 2016 (Trump over Hillary). We cannot count on it happening every year.

We must not self-indulgently avoid the reality that the Democrats did a better job of getting their people to vote than we did. They won the turnout war, and with it, the election.

There are new rules that govern our politics. The Democrats have learned them—and in many cases, invented them. Republicans and conservatives have not.

And that is why we lost. As Shakespeare wrote in *Julius Caesar*, "The fault, dear Brutus, is not in our stars, but in ourselves, that we are underlings."

And unless we learn the new rules and figure out how to beat the Democrats and the radical Left, we will lose again in 2022 and 2024.

If, indeed, we fail in those two contests, it won't matter how future elections turn out. Our nation and our democratic process will have been so fatally and irretrievably undermined that redemption will be impossible.

This book is divided into three parts:

- Part I lays out what we must do to stop the elections of 2022 and 2024 from being stolen, to make sure that more legal, eligible voters cast ballots for Republicans, and that their votes are not offset by a torrent of illegal ballots.

- Part II explains why our candidate in 2024 will be, and must be, Donald J. Trump. Accept no substitutes. Only he can put together the coalition that generated 74 million votes in 2020. And we don't want a bleached-out, kinder, nicer, gentler Donald Trump, either! We want and need the same Donald Trump who won in 2016, increased his vote share in 2020 by eleven million votes, and in between, was one of our truly great presidents.

- Part III examines our message. The Democrats are trying to transform America into a nation none of us will recognize. An economy dominated by inflation, where our savings, investments, pensions, 401(k)s, IRAs, and home values shrink each year as the dollar devalues. A country of porous borders and raging crime. They want to see a society as segregated by race as Mississippi or South Africa ever was, but this time with whites bearing the brunt of discrimination. A place where gender is a matter of opinion, and an accoutrement that can be changed as easily and whimsically as hair color. A nation dependent on China for its technology. A society where big tech, big media, and big brother tell us what to read and what to see. An unrecognizable land.

The Trump Revolution cannot succeed without Trump.
Will he run in 2024? You bet he will.
Will he be the GOP nominee? Absolutely.
Will he win the election? Yes.

But what if the Democrat (or the president) is not Biden at all, but Vice President Kamala Harris? Can we still win? Yes. How? You gotta read the book!

(By the way, Eileen and I wrote *The New York Times* bestselling book *Armageddon: How Trump Can Defeat Hillary*. It came out in the early summer of 2016, and we had completed it that spring. Our predictions came true. The white high-school-educated vote did turn out for Trump, and that made all the difference. Latinos did defect to Trump. Hillary was so mired in scandals of her own making that she tied herself in knots and could not articulate a message. So we know what we are talking about!)

PART I

Winning Under the New Rules

1

What Really Happened in 2020

To start our search, we must understand how the Democrats managed to turn out such a massive vote for one of the least electable people ever to run for president.

So frail, senile, and demented was Joe Biden that Democratic strategists used the threat of the COVID virus to keep their candidate in his basement, behind a mask, shielded from public view.

Nevertheless, the Democrats managed to win by expanding the size of the electorate.

Both parties worked furiously to bring out their vote. President Trump won eleven million more votes in 2020 than he got in 2016. But Biden was elected because he got fifteen million more votes than Hillary did.

The key change that impelled the huge rise in turnout was that the Democrats used the COVID virus pandemic to change the entire way elections are conducted.

The excuse for the massive change from in-person voting to casting ballots in absentia, or by mail, was the fear that bringing more than 150 million people out to vote in person on one day might kindle massive increases in case rate and deaths from COVID.

Even with the pandemic, roughly ninety million people chose to vote in person. If the dire warnings of Democrats were correct, we should have seen a spike in COVID deaths in the period immediately following Election Day.

Didn't happen. The COVID spike never took place. Election Day was November 3, 2020. During the first week of November 2020, 7,287 people died of COVID. The COVID spike never took place. In the second week of November, 8,014 died. In the third week, 10,684 passed away, and in the last week of November, the death toll was 10,273. No huge spike. At worst, a slight increase in deaths, more likely attributable to colder weather as winter approached.

If mail-in balloting didn't save a lot of lives, it sure fundamentally altered how people chose to vote, with almost half the electorate eschewing in-person voting.

It opened the door wide to all kinds of mischief.

- No need to go to the polls—absentee ballots came delivered to your front door by mail, from Democratic secretaries of state, or brought there by young, eager, bushy-tailed Democrats who canvassed door-to-door. Where formerly, voters had to offer an excuse to vote absentee, now, under the new rules, none was needed.

- Why wait for Election Day? Most states permitted early voting. Some as early as in September. And of course, the earlier the votes could be cast, the more time to return to the homes and apartments of those who had not yet voted, to urge them to do so.

- Of the votes cast in 2020, 42 percent came by mail, including many through special drop boxes placed on street corners in especially Democratic areas. Drop boxes—serviced by party workers, not federal postal employees—showed an abnormally high proportion of Biden votes.

- The new rules required that we take on faith the eligibility and the identity of each voter. Where ballots were mailed in, no identification was necessary, and often signatures were not properly verified. As a predictable result, potentially millions of people who had died or moved away were "voted for" by strangers.

- Even when the voters showed up in person, most swing states did not require photo IDs, so inspectors often had no idea who was really casting the ballot.

- In many states, ballots were "harvested" by party workers, collected en masse at events or by door-to-door canvassing, to be turned in later at the election offices. Sometimes votes for Trump did not make it through the process and never got turned in at the offices.

Arizona passed a law—before the 2020 election—prohibiting ballot harvesting. Only a family member or caregiver could cast a ballot on a voter's behalf. Predictably, the Democrats sued, arguing that the law violated the Voting Rights Act. But in July 2021, the US Supreme Court upheld the statute, citing the possibility of fraud.

Writing for the 6–3 majority, Justice Samuel Alito quoted the bipartisan Commission on Federal Election Reform chaired by former president Jimmy Carter and former secretary of state James Baker. The Carter-Baker Commission noted that "absentee balloting is *vulnerable to abuse* in several ways: . . . Citizens who vote at home, at nursing homes, at the workplace, or in church are more susceptible to pressure, overt and subtle, or to intimidation (emphasis added)."[1]

It has long been true that Republicans—with their more educated, motivated, industrious, patriotic, literate, and active voters—get out their vote more easily. But Democrats depend on getting downscale voters—minorities, teenagers, and couch potatoes—to vote. Paper ballots were made for them. If you don't care enough to go out and vote, hey, just mail it in!

The more apathetic, uninvolved, uninformed, low-motivation people who cast ballots, the greater the chances of a Democratic victory—a fact the Democrats knew well as they used the phony narrative of the COVID threat to induce mail-in voting.

Can we win in 2022 and 2024? Sure we can.

We must beat them under the new rules!

Don't pin your hopes on rolling the clock back to the days of limited turnouts. Embrace the high-turnout elections—just be sure we win.

After all, we Republicans have our share of couch potatoes, too! We don't need to cheat, or forge ballots, or help voters "cure" defective ballots. We can let the dead stay buried without casting votes in their names. Nor do we need to cast ballots in the names of those who have moved away.

We only need to dig deeper and focus on those who support us but didn't vote—people who took prosperity and jobs for granted and figured Trump had it in the bag.

We need to beat the Democrats by using the paper and absentee voting they pioneered in 2020. In 2020, about three in four absentee ballots were cast for Biden. In a pivotal state like Georgia, 80 percent of the paper ballots deposited in drop boxes (installed by Democrats and funded by Facebook founder Mark Zuckerberg) went for Biden.

Let's turn that around! No longer can we sit back and wait for Election Day! We must beat them on mail-in ballots and absentee votes every day of early voting. For us, now, Election Day is every day in October, and in some states, in September, too.

We have to scrounge for votes during the weeks and months before the election—as frantically as when the clock tells us the polls will close in two hours.

But Let's Not Kid Ourselves . . .

While ballot irregularities doubtless contributed to the Democratic victory in 2020, it was far from the whole story. Sure, there were many forged ballots cast in phony names, and many ballots that were altered by Democratic poll workers in the name of "curing" their defects. But the fact is, we ultimately lost because the Democrats got more legal, eligible voters to cast ballots than we did.

We must not lazily claim that cheating cost us the election, and assume that if we fix it by new legislation or administrative reforms or better poll watchers, that will magically produce Republican victories in 2022 and 2024. Nor dare we retreat into a nihilistic cynicism and refuse to vote at all. We see now what are the consequences of Democratic control.

Democrats won because they dug deeper to get votes by bringing ballots to their voters' front doors and collecting them—then and there—while we tried to get our people to go to the polls in person.

As any pizza delivery boy will tell you, home delivery beats going out, every time.

Paper ballots are here to stay, as are early voting and broader use of absentee ballots. We must adjust and win under the new rules.

How Did the Democrats Do It?

The Democrats won because:

- They persuaded Americans to vote by mail, not in person.
- They did not demand photo voter identification, and in some states, even barred inspectors from asking for it.
- They introduced no-excuse absentee voting. Anyone could vote without having to show up, or even to explain why they couldn't.
- They took advantage of laws allowing same-day registration to bring out millions of unregistered voters. Then they signed them up wholesale without checking identification, age, or residency. They made a mockery of voter registration—just show up and sign up.
- They used the court system to stop adequate verification of signatures on paper ballots, claiming that checking even obviously fraudulent signatures unfairly suppressed minority voting.
- They blocked efforts to trim from the rolls deceased voters and those who had moved out of state so they could fraudulently cast ballots in their names.
- They encouraged people to send in their ballots using special drop boxes erected only in Democratic neighborhoods.

Instead of using the Post Office, votes deposited in these drop boxes backed Biden by better than three to one. The ballots from these boxes were collected and brought to the vote tabulators by Democratic Party workers. The boxes themselves were financed privately by Democratic donors such as Facebook founder Mark Zuckerberg.

- They elected Democratic secretaries of state in key battleground states and used them to train inspectors to accept dubious paper ballots by the million.

All the while, Republicans played by the old rules, pushing for in-person voting and relying on the electoral system to screen out illegal ballots. The Republican Party worked, with astonishing success, to bring out their vote to the polls while the Democrats went door-to-door to encourage people to stay home and cast absentee ballots.

The Republicans worked their heads off, but home delivery— voting by paper ballots, at home—prevailed.

Now we have to win by using the new rules.

2

Elect Republican Secretaries of State

I F YOU HOPE TO win a ball game, take care to select fair umpires who won't cheat. In elections, the umpires are each state's secretary of state.

The 2020 election was lost in 2018, when Democrats elected compliant governors, radical leftist secretaries of state, and friendly attorneys general.

Although the voting machines will have different names of candidates in 2022, make no mistake, the election of 2024 will be decided by who wins these local offices in 2022!

The words attributed to Russian dictator Joseph Stalin were not lost on the Democratic Party. In fact, they became the party's motto in 2020. To quote: "It's not the people who vote that count; it's the people who count the votes" that matter.

Realizing the truth of this remark, the Democratic Party went all out to win elections for secretary of state in 2018, particularly in Michigan and Arizona. Their success in replacing Republicans with left-wing Democrats laid the basis for the successful efforts to carry those two states in 2020. In a third state—Pennsylvania—the secretary of state was appointed by the governor—who was a staunch Democrat—and in Georgia he was a RINO (Republican in name only) who did nothing to ensure an honest election.

Had Trump carried Georgia, Pennsylvania, Wisconsin, and Michigan, he would have won, 294–249, instead of losing, 237–306.

The election of 2020 was, in a real sense, won by the Democrats in 2018, when swing states elected their governors, attorneys general, and secretaries of state.

The Democrats knew that, in order to maximize the turnout of their voters in 2020, they had to build a network of complicit, election officials to cooperate—within the law, and outside it—to swell the Biden vote and diminish Trump's. They needed:

- People to overlook defects in Democratic paper and absentee ballots while tossing out any Republican ballots with any error, no matter how inconsequential.
- Election inspectors who would send absentee and paper ballots in the mail, disregarding whether they were requested or not. Then, with plenty of blank ballots distributed, they needed door-to-door canvassers to urge the voters, person-to-person, to fill them out for Biden.
- To change the policy on signature verification so that virtually any ballot marking would be acceptable in Democratic

precincts, but any similar vote in a Republican area would be tossed.

- To make sure that no photo identification was required anywhere along the process.
- To avoid purging the voter rolls of those who had died or moved away. Even if the voters didn't exist or had moved, the Democrats needed to be sure their names remained on the rolls, to be used—without photo ID—by impostors to cast their votes for Biden.
- Where paper ballots lacked a signature, weren't properly dated, or did not clearly make a preference known, they needed people who could assist the voter to "cure" the defect in the ballot so it could be counted . . . if it was for Biden.

The arbiters of all these tasks are the secretaries of each state. Elected in some states, and appointed in others (like Pennsylvania), they set and enforce the rules. No matter how scrupulous a state legislature is in enumerating the procedures it wants followed, the secretary of state wields the actual power over voting. (If a party didn't like the secretary of state's decisions, it could, of course, find recourse in the courts. But 2020 showed us all how illusory that power is.)

Florida's secretary of state, Republican Katherine Harris consistently ruled in favor of Bush in the disputed election of 2000. She says that she was upholding the law scrupulously but her rulings were enough to heighten Democratic determination to control secretaries of state offices around the country. It is secretaries of state who set the rules; govern how paper ballots are treated; employ, select, train, and instruct the election workers; and establish the ground rules for how to treat observers from both parties.

After the 2000 election, the Democrats became obsessed with controlling the election machinery in swing states. Blaming Gore's defeat on Republican control of the governorship and the Florida secretary of state, the Democrats set out to take over the election apparatus while Republicans complacently paid no attention.

In 2014, they formed iVote, a Democratic organization dedicated to controlling and manipulating the voting process in swing states throughout America. iVote knew how important secretaries of state were in the forty states where they are the chief election officers.

As iVote explains on its website, "While it's a little-known office, state-level secretaries of state are the most important official in determining who votes and who doesn't." The problem, iVote said, was that two-thirds of all secretaries of state were Republican.

But iVote saw that these Republican secretaries of state in crucial battleground states could be easily picked off.

The job itself tends to attract few candidates. Nobody wants to run for it. The normal duties of the office are inherently boring. The secretary licenses business, health, and real estate professionals; maintains registration and financial information for thousands of charities; maintains corporate filings; and sanctions certain professional sports such as boxing, kickboxing, and wrestling. He or she is also the keeper of the great seal of the state (or commonwealth).

The only attractive or interesting task is to supervise elections.

Few candidates vie for the office each election year, and they typically spend little on their campaigns.

Because the elections for secretary of state are so low-profile, and the job so intrinsically uninteresting, they tend to attract weak candidates who are poorly funded. Until the elections of 2020 made them so controversial and important, few candidates for the office spent much to get elected. The position is hardly ever a springboard to higher office, and generates little attention and few donors.

Stepping into this vacuum, the Democrats recruited candidates to run whose leftist, radical credentials were well-established. Funded by George Soros, iVote spent $6 million in the elections of 2018 to help its secretary of state candidates win.

This level of spending—seemingly minor in comparison with the $14 billion spent overall in the 2020 elections—nevertheless, overwhelmed their Republican opponents in key races in Michigan and Arizona, setting up the opportunity for expanding the electorate in 2020, by any means, fair or foul.

In their campaigns for secretary of state, Democratic candidates emphasized the importance of allowing people to vote by mail, and of opposing efforts to "suppress the turnout," such as signature verification, voter identification, and proof of residence.

The Center for American Progress Fund, a pro-Democrat civil rights organization, listed the challenges facing secretaries of state in 2020. "The United States is simultaneously confronting three wrenching challenges: the deadly COVID-19 pandemic, deep economic upheaval, and systemic racism—issues that disproportionately affect African Americans. Compounding these critical issues is the racial discrimination that pervades the US voting system and silences the voices of the communities that are most affected."[1]

To those who bought into the phony narrative of widespread voter suppression in minority communities, the work of radical secretaries of state to reduce the obstacles to voting seemed reasonable. When they loosened requirements that voters be registered, have photo identification, or sign in properly, they said they were just remedying past injustice. But who knew that they were really preparing to determine the outcome of a presidential election?

But just changing the theoretical procedures and balloting regulations, by itself, would not have been enough to permit hundreds of thousands of questionable ballots to be accepted and tabulated. Even compliant secretaries of state could not have done the job. The Democratic Party needed new people to man each polling place, each voter identification table, and each signature verification desk—their own people, their own partisans, to tilt the process sufficiently for their purposes.

And that's where Facebook CEO Mark Zuckerberg fit into their plans. Zuckerberg spent $419.5 million on the 2020 campaign. But, as the *New York Post* reported, the funding had nothing to do with regular, routine electioneering expenses like advertising, social media, or rallies. The *Post* explained that, "it had to do with financing the infiltration of election offices at the city and county level by left-wing activists and using those offices as a platform to implement preferred administrative practices, voting methods and data-sharing agreements, as well as to launch intensive outreach campaigns in areas heavy with Democratic voters."

The newspaper noted that "analysis conducted by our team demonstrates this money significantly increased Joe Biden's vote margin in key swing states. In places like Georgia, where Biden won by 12,000 votes, and Arizona, where he won by 10,000, the spending likely put him over the top."

The *Post* opined: "This unprecedented merger of public election offices with private resources and personnel is an acute threat to our republic and should be the focus of electoral reform efforts moving forward." And it concluded, "the 2020 election wasn't stolen—it was likely bought by one of the world's wealthiest and most powerful men."[2]

Zuckerberg's army, acting in close coordination with partisan secretaries of state, did the nitty gritty work on election day.

But first, the Democrats needed to control the secretary of state offices in swing states.

Michigan

Their most important victory came in Michigan, where the radical Left elected Jocelyn Benson, a forty-three-year-old ultra-leftist who defeated Mary Trevor Lang, the Republican incumbent.

Benson studied at Oxford University, where she conducted research into the "sociological implications of white supremacy and neo-Nazism."[3] She also worked for the Southern Poverty Law Center, where she continued her efforts to probe white supremacist and neo-Nazi organizations. She spent almost $2 million on her race for secretary of state, with iVote spending just under $1 million more on her behalf.

Benson's election began to pay dividends to her Democratic sponsors almost immediately when she was able to send out absentee ballots to 7.7 million people in Michigan, almost none of whom had actually asked for them. In Wayne County (Detroit), for example, of the 566,788 absentee ballots cast, according to official records, 203,311—36 percent—had not been requested by the voters.

But once these absentee ballots had been filled in, and arrived at the secretary of state's office, Benson's real mischief began. Michigan state law requires that absentee ballot signatures be scrutinized closely, but Benson instructed her poll workers—perhaps paid with Zuckerberg's money—to presume the accuracy of the signatures and only throw out ballots that either lacked a signature entirely, or where the signature was an obvious forgery.

On March 16, 2021—well after the election—Judge Christopher Murray, of the state's Court of Claims, ruled that Benson had violated state law by the "guidance" she had issued to her election workers. He found that Benson "did not follow the proper rule-making process when instructing voting clerks in October [2020] to presume the accuracy of absentee ballot signatures,"[4] and added that "the presumption is found nowhere in state law." He held that "the mandatory presumption goes beyond the realm of mere advice and direction, and instead is a substantive directive that adds to the pertinent signature-matching standards." Judge Murray wrote that "Benson issued the rules without following the process for creating a rule under state and federal law, thus violating the state's Administrative Procedures Act."[5]

Unfortunately, the judge's decision came five months too late to affect the outcome of the 2020 election.

Having vested the ballot counters with such authority over signature verification, Benson then made sure that the boards that counted the ballots were heavily weighted with Democrats and had few Republicans involved in the process.

When a study found that Benson had packed the boards with Democrats, the Wayne County Board of Canvassers voted unanimously to order an audit of the county's election results.

Despite the order, Benson never conducted the audit.

Arizona

In Arizona, too, Biden's surprising victory can be directly linked to Democratic secretary of state Katie Hobbs, who beat Republican Steve Gaynor in 2018. Hobbs, a social worker for twenty years, may have learned how to use absentee and late-arriving mail ballots to fudge the voting system from her own experience when she herself got elected in 2018.

The tsunami that was Arizona's election in 2020 had been preceded by a similar one in 2018. You would think the Republican Party would have learned from that experience and prepared better to prevent a repeat in 2020, but go figure!

In 2018, the Republican Senate candidate Martha McSally beat Democrat Kyrsten Sinema in their race to fill a vacant US Senate seat. That is, McSally won on election night. Then, over the next week, hundreds of thousands of early, absentee, and provisional ballots were reviewed, contested, and counted—and at the end of it all, Arizonans found out that Sinema had won.

And the exact same thing happened in Hobbs's race for secretary of state. Republican Steve Gaynor led on election night by 40,000 votes, only to lose by 20,252 votes when the final count was certified.

Chris Buskirk, writing in *Real Clear Politics,* explains that, in race after race that year in Arizona, "Republicans wound up on the losing end." In all of these races, he writes, the Republican led on election night, only to lose his lead when the final certified count came a week or more later." He asks the obvious questions: "How could this happen? Was it legitimate, or is there a real reason for concern over the integrity of the election? Contributing to the suspicion is not only the lead changes, but the substantial amount of time between Election Day and the certification of the vote. Most people understand intuitively that the more time that elapses, the more opportunity there is for cheating."[6]

What an opportunity to peer into the future and avert the worst that the Republican Party had in the months before the 2020 election season! The Democrats used the same underhanded tactics to win the Senate seat and the secretary of state elections of 2018 in Arizona that they used to carry that state, and many others, in 2020. If only we had paid closer attention!

So widespread and credible were the charges of cheating in the 2020 election, that the Arizona State Senate commissioned an independent audit of the voting in Maricopa County—Arizona's largest—to determine whether the election was honest or not. When the audit results were released in September 2021, Democratic publicists pounced on them to point out that they showed that Biden did indeed carry Arizona by an even larger margin than reported on Election Day.

But an examination of the audit report itself shows that Biden only won due to massive cheating. The earlier reports that said Biden's win had been confirmed by the audit result, was due to the deliberate failure of the left-wing media to distinguish the results of the recount from those of the audit. They are not synonyms. The recount, in this case, simply counted the votes again without even attempting to determine their validity. Unsurprisingly, the recount showed no change in the numbers. But when the independent auditors examined the validity of the votes themselves, they found massive fraud:

- 23,344 mail-in ballots came from voters who did not live at the home addresses from which they were registered. No one with the same last name was found at the address in a follow-up personal visit by the auditors. Some of the addresses given by voters turned out to be empty lots. The Post Office had been instructed not to forward mailings designed to verify voter addresses so the state could keep track of who had moved. This finding raises the question of whether these "ghost" voters existed at all or still lived in state.

- 17,322 duplicate ballots were counted—some with voters casting the same ballot three or four times. A quarter of these duplicate votes came in after Election Day, when news reports emphasized how desperately Biden needed to carry the state.

- 9,041 people may have voted twice. The auditors report that "in most of these instances," an individual was sent one ballot but had two ballots received (from them) on different dates.

- 5,295 voters may have voted in two different counties. Auditors found that many voters who had voted with the same first, middle, and last names and the same birth dates, in two different counties.

- 3,432 more ballots were counted than people were recorded as having voted.

- Where ballots were damaged or improperly marked, a duplicate was made and counted that preserved the voter's intent. In all, 25,965 original ballots were sent out to be duplicated, but 29,557 were returned. Where did the other 2,592 ballots come from?

- 2,081 votes were counted from people who had moved out of state in the thirty days before the election.

- 198 votes came from voters who had registered after the October 15th deadline.

- 282 ballots were cast in the names of the dead. RIP.

In all, the audit revealed serious issues with 53,000 votes. Biden carried Arizona by 10,000 votes.

Part of the answer lies in Maricopa County, where the highly partisan Recorder Adrian Fontes may have ignored or fudged the signature-verification process for early ballots, which accounted for roughly 80 percent of all votes in 2018. That's nearly two million unsecured ballots. Even though Republicans nominally controlled the County Board of Supervisors, Adrian Fontes was a Democrat, and it was he who was in charge.

While Biden may have carried Arizona under the rules Secretary of State Hobbs and Maricopa County Recorder Adrian Fontes established, the future looks brighter for Republicans in Arizona. In the same 2020 election that Biden "won," Fontes lost his bid for re-election to Republican Stephen Richer, a business-man who has never held public office before, and vows to clean up the mess Fontes left behind.

Meanwhile, the Supreme Court finally stepped in to demand reform of ballot harvesting in Arizona, where party workers were allowed to go into the district to collect paper ballots and then turn them in to country officials.

Ballot harvesting was most common where Democrats could bring pressure on voters to support their candidates. For example, in public housing projects, community centers in minority neighborhoods, Native-American reservations, and nursing homes, the subtle pressure of a Democratic campaign worker on the doorstep can influence people to vote for their candi-date. In some cases, the Democratic Party worker was accom-panied on his or her rounds by some local honcho who could, in effect, coerce the voter to support the party. In public hous-ing projects, influential neighbors brought around the ballot boxes, pressing for votes for Biden. In nursing homes, physi-cally dependent people were frequently solicited in the presence of their caregiver. On reservations and in community centers, local leaders or managers often helped to harvest ballots.

There was the further problem that it was questionable whether a ballot for the other side would ever even be submitted. And of course, the process made a mockery of ballot secrecy.

The Democratic Party sued to overturn the new law, and on July 1, 2021, the US Supreme Court ruled in favor of the state law banning ballot harvesting (*Brnovich, Attorney General of Arizona, et. al. v. Democratic National Committee, et. al.*). The Court's decision has enormous significance. Not only does it outlaw a frequent Democratic tactic, but it sets a clear precedent establishing the state sovereignty over elections, specified in the Constitution.

Georgia

Sometimes it isn't enough to have a Republican governor and secretary of state if they turn out to be RINOs like the current governor, Brian Kemp, and the secretary of state, Brad Raffensperger. In fact, there are no two people in the United States who are more responsible for the injustice of the election of 2020 than Kemp and Raffensperger. Their bad decisions, and their stubborn tenacity in defending them, doomed not only President Trump's chances in Georgia, but also those of Republican senators David Purdue and Kelly Loeffler, handing control of the Senate to the Democrats.

After the damage was done, and Biden had carried Georgia, and Purdue and Loeffler were defeated, and the US Senate was handed to the Democrats, Kemp tried to cover himself by backing a great election-reform bill that passed, and will block Georgia Democratic shenanigans in the future. But the fact remains that Kemp and Raffensperger are more responsible for the catastrophe of 2020 than any other Republicans in America.

I can only hope and pray that Georgia Republicans are not fooled and vote against Kemp in the Republican Primary for governor. The current Republican front runner challenging Kemp in the primary is Vernon Jones, an extremely impressive African American who was the head of DeKalb County and a former Democrat. And a vote for Congressman Jody Hice, running against Raffensperger, is a must for anyone who wants Trump elected again—or for a fair election in Georgia.

As with so many of the election irregularities that marred the 2020 race, the controversy over Georgia's electoral votes began in 2018, when Georgia House of Representatives Minority Leader Stacey Abrams lost the gubernatorial election to incumbent secretary of state—and future governor—Republican Brian Kemp. In that bitter contest, Kemp prevailed by sixty thousand votes, but Abrams refused to concede, and litigated in federal court.

She based her case on the fact that, as secretary of state, Kemp had canceled the registrations of 1.4 million voters, either because they had moved away, died, had not voted in several previous elections, or had failed to respond to mailings requesting confirmation of their eligibility. The media called it "the largest mass disenfranchisement in US history."[7]

Since many of those dropped from the rolls were minorities, Abrams sued under the federal Voting Rights Act.

While these voters had been technically purged from the voting rolls, they could have easily restored their voter registrations and cast ballots if they had wanted to.

Charles Bullock, a professor of political science at the University of Georgia, explained that "all the person had to do [to restore their registration] is show up with their photo ID, which everyone has to have, and they would've been allowed to vote."[8]

However, after the lawsuit had dragged on for over a year, and preliminary motions had gone against the state, the new secretary of state, Brad Raffensperger, and the new governor, Brian Kemp, agreed to settle the suit. In the consent decree, they pledged to use only one inspection—not the previously required two—to verify voter signatures on absentee and mailed-in ballots, and to be less strict in purging the voter rolls.

This agreement laid the basis for the controversy surrounding the 2020 presidential election and the subsequent runoff for two Senate seats.

Against the backdrop of the unfavorable publicity stemming from the Abrams lawsuit, both Kemp and Raffensperger were loath to enforce even necessary safeguards such as vigorous signature verification, identity checks, and cleansing the voter rolls to remove those who had moved away or passed away. Their reticence opened up massive opportunities for Democratic campaign workers to count highly questionable ballots.

In the three months between the November election and the January runoff for the two Senate seats, leaders of the Georgia General Assembly—that was in Republican hands—sought to audit the results of the presidential election, and as importantly, close the opportunity for further mischief in the runoff elections two months later. However, while the GOP had majorities in both Houses that were eager to act, Governor Kemp refused to call them into special session, thereby ensuring the election of radical Democrats Raphael Warnock and John Ossoff to the Senate, tipping control to the Democrats. Had Kemp only listened to his fellow Republicans and called them into special session, they would have likely passed the same kind of excellent, rigorous election reform bill back then that they have since passed. This would have foreclosed the Democratic tactics that led to Biden's victory in Georgia, and then delivered two Senate seats to the Democrats, and with it, control of the US Senate. But his failure to act—God knows why—allowed the Democrats to get away with precisely the kind of tactics they used in the November election, and predictably, both Senate seats went Democrat. It's a perfect example of the old adage, "Fool me once, shame on you. Fool me twice, shame on me."

Shame on Governor Kemp!

The solution is obvious: we must elect more reliable Republicans to both offices—governor and secretary of state—in the elections of 2022. If we let the incumbents win again, or be replaced by Democrats, we will undoubtedly lose Georgia once more.

We should see the Georgia elections of 2022 as the equivalent of a presidential contest, since it is unlikely that a Republican will be elected president in 2024 if we don't change both the governor and the secretary of state.

Hice, who is opposing Raffensperger with the vigorous support of Trump, says that the Republicans would have won in Georgia had the elections been conducted "fairly." He notes that Raffensperger sent out seven hundred thousand ballot applications to "illegal voters," and that there was obviously some "fraud mixed up in there."

"I believe if there was a fair election, it would be a different outcome," Hice told CNN. When asked whether he believed Trump won Georgia, he replied, "Absolutely. I do not believe for one moment that Georgia is a blue state."[9]

Pennsylvania

Nowhere were the election irregularities more blatant than in Pennsylvania, where the secretary of state is not elected, but appointed by the governor. There, Democratic governor Tom Wolf appointed dedicated ultra-leftist Kathy Boockvar to be the secretary. Boockvar used her position ruthlessly to deliver the vote count to Biden.

- Pennsylvania kept the polls open for absentee and mail-in ballots for four days after Election Day, despite a state law prohibiting late voting, and a US Supreme Court decision allowing it for only three days after the election.
- Pennsylvania permitted Democratic poll workers to "cure" (i.e., alter or forge) defective paper ballots so that they would be counted. This process of "curing" was demonstrated to be taking place only in largely Democratic precincts.
- During the election itself and subsequent recounts, Pennsylvania ensured that Republican inspectors would be kept far away from the actual vote counting, and unable to see what was going on, despite state law to the contrary.
- While in 2016, a full 1 percent of all paper and absentee ballots had been rejected by election inspectors for irregularities in signatures and voter eligibility, the rejection rate in 2020 fell to only 0.03 percent, a thirty-three-times lower rate. Election officials, encouraged by the governor and the secretary of state, were notably lax in their standards for accepting paper ballots, about three-quarters of which went for Biden.

Kathy Boockvar is no longer Pennsylvania's secretary of state. She was forced to resign two months after the 2020 election when her malfeasance and incompetence led to the defeat of a ballot measure that would have extended the statute of limitations on child sexual abuse claims. Her department failed to advertise properly that the constitutional amendment in question was on the ballot.

Governor Wolf named Veronica Degraffenreid to be acting secretary. Degraffenreid had joined the department under Boockvar as special advisor on election modernization.

Fortunately for our democracy, Wolf is term-limited and cannot seek re-election in 2022. The stakes are high in Pennsylvania, where there will also be a vacant US Senate seat up for grabs. But a Republican victory in the 2022 election for governor will be a key prerequisite for winning back the White House.

An astute political analyst, Dan Greenfield, summed up how the Democrats laid the basis for winning the 2020 presidential election in 2018. "In 2018," he wrote in Frontpagemag.com, "Democrats struck a calculated blow against the electoral system, one that paid off tremendously when a pandemic arrived that allowed them to carry out their wildest plans." But these plans were already in the pipeline long before the pandemic provided an excuse.

Undeterred, iVote is still pushing for new legislation to institutionalize the practice of stealing elections. Its agenda includes automatic voter registration, pre-registration for teenagers, and expansion of vote-by-mail. It fervently opposes voter ID requirements, signature verification, and cross-checking voter-registration lists with other state databases.

Bashing Republican efforts to ensure fair and honest elections, California Secretary of State Alejandro Padilla called them "about as small-d undemocratic and un-American as it gets."

In the end, the iVote strategy worked wonders. Every single state that had a Democratic secretary of state went for Biden. But the real Democratic plan for jimmying the election of 2024 is to pass HR 1, a massive federal power grab to take over the election system from the states.

3

Stop HR 1

O<small>N THE VERY FIRST</small> day of the 2021–2022 legislative session, House Speaker Nancy Pelosi introduced HR 1. Traditionally, the speaker can introduce her most important legislative priority and give it the bill number HR 1. And in the Senate, newly minted Majority Leader Chuck Schumer introduced a companion bill, labeled S 1.

Simply put, together, these bills can end democracy as we know it in the United States.

They have essentially codified all of the tactics of the Democrats in 2020, and legalized them. Instead of correcting and punishing those who break election laws, HR 1 legitimizes their conduct.

It's as if, after the robbery of a grocery store, Congress passed a new law legalizing burglary. HR 1 and S 1 would enshrine into law the shenanigans of the Democrats in the 2020 election. Their obvious hope is that these rules will become the new norm in American politics.

HR 1 breezed through the House on March 3, 2021, just weeks after Election Day, but it is stalled in the Senate by a Republican filibuster. Democrats were intent on defeating any filibuster by changing Senate rules to prohibit them, but Senators Joe Manchin (D-WV) and Krysten Sinema (D-AZ) appear to have saved the day by affirming their refusal to support these bills or to back curbs on filibusters against them.

However, in announcing his opposition to S 1, Manchin said he would consider supporting the John Lewis Voting Rights Act, an earlier proposal on the topic advanced by the Left and named after the late civil rights movement hero-turned-congressman John Lewis.

Obviously, Manchin's move will open the door to a provision-by-provision review of S 1 and HR 1 to see what might be incorporated in the John Lewis Act and still pass the Senate.

So let's take a minute to review what the Democrats are trying to do in these bills, and what are the election-stealing practices they want to legalize. (Bear in mind that, even if we stop them from superseding state laws and passing these laws legalizing fraud, they will keep knocking at the Senate door, and will pass these changes in blue states, assuring that they stay in control).

Superficially, some of the provisions of HR 1 seem benign, and even constructive. But in the context of today's politics, we can appreciate just how toxic they would be if enacted.

Stripping States of Control Over Elections

When our federal Constitution was adopted, a movement led by New York State Governor George Clinton opposed ratification. Clinton argued that giving the federal government control over elections made it possible to establish a dictatorship or a monarchy. To assuage his concerns, the Constitution drafter James Madison included a provision giving state legislatures the power to regulate elections.

Article 1, Section 4, Clause 1 of the Constitution reads: "The Times, Places and Manner of holding Elections for Senators and Representatives, shall be prescribed in each State by the Legislature thereof; but Congress may at any time make or alter such Regulations, except as to the Place of choosing Senators."

However, based on overwhelming evidence of discrimination against minorities in the former states of the Confederacy, Congress passed the Voting Rights Act of 1965, imposing requirements on those specific states to prevent discrimination—in effect, over-riding the constitutional provision. (The courts ruled that it was constitutional to do so, since the discrimination was itself a violation of the Fifteenth Amendment, assuring Blacks the right to vote.)

Specifically, the Act required the prior approval of the US Department of Justice before those former Confederate states could adopt any changes in regulations about voting procedures, qualifications for voter registration, or alterations in the lines of congressional districts.

In 2013, the US Supreme Court threw out the Voting Rights Act, holding that there was no longer sufficient evidence of discrimination in those states to subject them to the pre-clearance provisions of the Act.

Both HR 1 and the John Lewis Act would reverse the 2013 decision and apply the Voting Rights Act's pre-clearance requirements to all fifty states, even where there is no evidence of racial discrimination.

So it would totally federalize election regulation.

It would vest the power to draw district lines and adopt other regulations about elections in the federal Department of Justice and the US attorney general, appointed by the president.

So if President Biden and his appointees were to disapprove of the congressional lines drawn by state legislatures throughout the country, HR 1 would give them the power to throw out those lines and replace them with ones that they would draw. That power would, in effect, give them the ability to control congressional elections and ensure that the Democrats always win.

Voter Registration

HR 1 essentially says, "If it's alive and it moves, register it to vote!" Democrats see no reason why anybody who lives here is not permitted to vote. They see voter registration as a formality designed only to bar people from exercising the franchise.

Undoubtedly, if they had their way, there would be no such thing as voter registration. Anyone who showed up at a polling place or mailed in a ballot would be permitted to vote. They believe that requirements like citizenship or residency are just artificial barriers—impediments to the franchise—that should be bypassed and ignored.

So HR 1 requires same-day registration. Anyone who comes in person to vote, or mails in a ballot, could be registered to vote, right then and there.

And remember that Democrats are staunchly opposed to requiring photo identification to register to vote. So we are supposed to sign everybody up to vote without verifying their name, address, citizenship, age, or length of residency, and without having their photo in the files. This allergy to documentation and proof, combined with same-day registration—which allows no time for authentication—and essentially eliminates any controls on who votes or how often they do so.

It will make voting in American elections much like voting in the selection of All-Star teams in Major League Baseball (MLB). A few years ago, MLB decided to permit fans to vote on who should play in the All-Star games. Ballots are distributed at all games, and fans routinely vote multiple times for their favorites. Eventually, MLB limited the number of times one person could vote, but it never enforced the rule.

That's how we will end up choosing our president and Congress if the Left has its way!

Lurking in the background are upward of fifteen million illegal immigrants now living in the United States. Because the Left is certain that these immigrants would vote heavily Democratic if they could, the goal of the Democrats in election "reforms" is to get these fifteen-million-plus people onto the voting rolls, which would give them enough new voters to tip any election to the Democratic Party.

Meanwhile, Democrats—notably, including the president— are doing all they can to weaken our immigration controls in order to increase the number of illegal immigrants. Once they are here, Democrats want to smuggle them onto the voting rolls.

Already, particularly in California, illegal immigrants are being given a limited right to vote in school board elections and other local contests where federal rules do not apply. Democrats hope to pass legislation granting these illegal immigrants a path to citizenship and voting, but until they do, they are trying to change the registration procedures to make it easier for them to cheat and let illegals vote anyway—a core motivation behind HR 1.

The New York City Council has take the ultimate step to blur any distinction between citizens and non-citizens in allowing the vote. It has passed a local law allowing non-citizens to vote in municipal elections, an action that expands New York City's electorate by up to a million voters. Democrats hope that this new law will be a precedent to enfranchise them in federal presidential and congressional elections.

HR 1 would also set up a system of automatic and involuntary voter registration. If someone were to file their personal data with a state agency—be it in an application for a driver's license, food stamps, welfare, unemployment, or worker's compensation—they would automatically be enrolled as voters. Linking government handouts with voter registration is a sneaky way to make sure that those who depend on public welfare in one form or another will be able to vote to continue or raise the payments.

The proposed law would also permit online voter registration, ensuring that no identity checks would be possible. Election officials would have to take the applicant's word for his bona fides.

And HR 1 would start them young—when they would be more likely to be idealistic Democrats, before life teaches them reality. It would let sixteen- and seventeen-year-olds preregister so they'd be on the rolls when they turn eighteen. Some Democrats have proposed lowering the voting age to sixteen, and we can assume that will be their next step.

Once you're registered, you're registered forever. HR 1 bans states from dropping voters just because they haven't voted in years. The presumption, of course, is that many of those who have not voted in a number of past elections might have moved or passed away. Since there is no automatic requirement that people report moving out of state to the election authorities, and nobody "unregisters" when they move out, but just register in a new location, this purging is the only realistic way of keeping the voter rolls up to date.

And boy do they need updating. The Election Integrity Project California (EIPCa) reports that "thirteen of the state's counties have more registered voters than eligible citizens—totaling over one million ineligible registrants."[1]

The Federal Election Assistance Commission revealed, in 2020, that there were 378 US counties where voter registration rates exceeded 100 percent of the adult population—more voters than people. By this methodology alone, the Commission estimated that there were at least (!) 2.5 million ineligible voters.

The National Voter Registration Act (NVRA)—also known as the Motor-Voter law, because it links voter registration with driver's license issuance—requires states to remove from the rolls people who have died or moved, or are otherwise ineligible to vote, from the rolls. But states, eager to augment their political power and beef up their congressional representation, just don't comply with this particular law.

The NVRA does a great deal to protect voters from being dropped from the rolls. A state must send a notice to the voter that his or her name is about to be deleted from the voting rolls. The mailing must include a postage-prepaid and pre-addressed return card, on which the person may state his or her current address. Only if the card is not returned, and the voter has sat out two consecutive federal elections, may he or she be removed. And then, if he or she goes to a polling location and swears out an affidavit establishing eligibility, he or she is automatically re-enrolled.

But that's not good enough for HR 1, which bans dropping voters for failure to vote.

Why are the Democrats so solicitous about protecting people from being dropped? Not to protect their rights, but to keep them on the voter rolls so campaign workers can cast ghost ballots in their names—a fraud made easier by the ban on requiring photo IDs.

The state of North Carolina matched its voter records from the 2016 election with those of other states and found 75,000 people who lived in other states and had voted there, but who had the same first, middle, and last names and birth dates as various North Carolina voters who had voted in the 2016 election.

Coincidence? Trump said, "No way," so he set up a national commission to do a similar match nationwide. But Democratic secretaries of state refused to provide the commission with the necessary data. And rather than face endless litigation, the commission was disbanded.

Stacking Federal Elections Commission

One of the few agencies in our government that is genuinely bipartisan is the Federal Elections Commission (FEC), composed of three representatives of each political party. While the Commission's composition ensures many 3–3 ties, it also stops it from stacking the rules to favor one of the parties.

HR 1 changes the law to make the FEC a partisan institution. It gives the president the power to appoint a seventh commissioner, giving the party in power a 4–3 majority.

No longer will decisions about election funding, reporting, procedures, and practices be impartial; they will be totally partisan. The neutral umpire now in charge will be replaced by one of the coaches from the president's team.

Early Voting

Not all of HR 1 is horrific. Among its good provisions is a requirement that states provide for two weeks of early in-person voting, and that they standardize the hours for opening and closing polling places.

There is a tendency among Republicans to oppose early voting. But why? I don't get it. There's nothing wrong with early voting, and it increases the turnout. It does give political parties plenty of time to pull out reluctant voters to the polls, or to get them to send in ballots, but so what? As long as it's the same for both parties, what's the problem? It just means that the Republican Party has to work harder at producing a vote. But there's nothing wrong with that.

Letting Former Felons Vote

In many states, convicted felons can't vote. In others, they have to wait until they have served their sentences or have waited out their period of probation. The Democrats call this process "felony disenfranchisement." But states have a legitimate reason for excluding those who have flouted our laws from helping to shape them.

Only DC, Maine, and Vermont permit incarcerated felons to vote. On the other hand, eighteen states ban voting during incarceration but automatically restore it upon release. Nineteen states also ban felon voting during parole or probation, and eleven ban voting indefinitely for some crimes.

Democratic-allied groups estimate that 5.2 million Americans are "locked out" of voting because of prior felony convictions, three-quarters of whom are Black.[2]

HR 1 denies states the right to exclude former felons not actually in prison from the right to vote. Democrats gleefully expect to receive the votes of all the former criminals they can sign up. They're probably right.

Washington, DC, is one of the jurisdictions that let felons vote. In 2021, the District actually elected a guy serving a twenty-six-year sentence for murder, to a public office. Once DC gave felons the right to vote (even while they were in prison), the DC City Council drew a district that included Joel Caston's jail, where he's doing time for ambushing and murdering a man in the city's Anacostia neighborhood. The cops had found a "speed loader" (used to load ammo rapidly) under his mattress, replete with extra cartridges.

Caston ran, was elected, and is now serving as a commissioner on DC's Advisory Neighborhood Commission, which advises the DC City Council on liquor licenses and public safety questions. He'll serve a two-year term—while still serving his other term of twenty-six years in prison—and get a laptop, an office in the prison, an email account, and eight hours a day to service his district.

Caston won a five-way contest in which his four opponents were also inmates at his jail.

Caston just might be the only incumbent, elected official in America to favor term limits!

Such is the new world of the Democratic Party!

Redistricting

With Republican majorities in sixty-one of America's ninety-nine state legislative chambers (Nebraska is unicameral), HR 1 would require that non-partisan commissions draw the new lines for House districts after the 2030 census.

But more importantly, it gives the Department of Justice (DOJ) the right to pre-clear new districts, effectively ending the right of states to control them.

Of course, the US attorney general, who heads the DOJ, is a partisan appointed by the president. So effectively, HR 1 gives the president and his appointee the power to draw House district lines without even getting input from states' elected legislators. There would be nothing to stop him from such partisan gerrymandering that his party would win all congressional elections. All the time!

HR 1 and S 1 must be defeated at all costs!

Pass Real Election Reforms in State Legislatures

In the aftermath of the 2020 wipeout, democracy seems impaired, and our freedoms imperiled. But federalism can still save us. At the state level, even in important swing states, reforms that run directly contrary to the nefarious provisions of HR 1 are making their way through the various state legislatures.

The prospects for real reform are bright in Arizona, Florida, Iowa, Georgia, and Ohio, where Republicans control both the governor and both Houses of the legislature.

In Nevada and Colorado, where Democrats control it all, the odds of any fair reform are almost nil.

But whether fair election laws can pass in Michigan, North Carolina, Pennsylvania, and Wisconsin—where Republicans run the legislature, but Democrats control the governorships—is more problematic.

These four states—which have sixty-one electoral votes—hold the key to the 2024 presidential election. If Republicans can sweep them, we are likely to see a change in the White House.

In Pennsylvania, Democratic Governor Tom Wolf is term-limited, so his seat will be open. Pennsylvania elections are always close, but the state has a tradition of alternating control, so no party keeps power for too long. Hopefully, this trend will continue.

We will also face uphill battles in Michigan, Wisconsin, and North Carolina, where governors Gretchen Whitmer (MI), Tony Evers (WI), and Roy Cooper (NC) will run for a second term.

Michigan Governor Whitmer trailed her likely Republican opponent, former Detroit Police Chief James Craig, by six points in a September 2021 poll.

And in Wisconsin, an August 24, 2021 poll showed incumbent Democratic governor, Tony Evers, just edging out the likely Republic candidate, former Lt. Governor Rebecca Kleefisch, by 39–38.

In retrospect, the Democratic gubernatorial victories in Michigan, Wisconsin, and North Carolina—all in 2018—were part of a premeditated plan to win the 2020 presidential election by any means possible. Recapturing these governorships is key to reclaiming the White House.

PART II

It Has to Be Trump

4

Donald Trump: One of Our Great Presidents

Donald J. Trump has been one of America's great presidents. Not just good, but great. Part of his greatness is reflected in his immense achievements. But the greater tribute is how he defied almost every establishment in the country to achieve what America needed, and our people demanded.

He defied the economic establishment by getting Congress to pass a massive tax cut, skillfully crafted to aim at the middle class, the working poor, and small businesses. The establishment said cut taxes on the wealthy, and it will trickle down to the rest of society. But Trump knew that trickle-down doesn't always happen. So he made sure his tax cuts were the first in recent history to target the lower middle class—the working class. Trump signed a law giving a tax credit of $2,000 per child, and changed tax rates so the lower-income people did not even have to file returns.

Then he disregarded the complaints of the pro-China lobby and globalists, distributed among the corporate and foreign policy elites, by holding Beijing accountable for its unfair trade practices through massive and highly effective trade sanctions.

The establishment wanted free trade, just like Adam Smith prescribed. But Trump insisted that we use our power to stop China from cheating, and force it to compete on a level playing field.

The establishment cautioned him not to mess with China. They said that we owe them so much money, they could pull the plug on us anytime they want to. But as a businessman, Trump understood that it is we who have the upper hand because we buy three times as much from China as they buy from us. And the debt? Trump realized that our debt to China made them dependent on us, not the other way around. After all, *we* are the ones sitting on *their* money. (Remember the saying that if you borrow $100,000 from a bank, the bank owns you, but if you borrow $10 million, you control the bank.)

The establishment wanted free flow of labor and open borders. But Trump demanded that we keep illegal immigrants out. He said that if we have millions of people willing to work for very little, there's no way the middle class can move up in wages.

The environmental establishment wanted to scrap fossil fuels and go to wind and solar energy. But Trump pointed out that we have worked hard for forty years to be energy independent. So why would we give that power away? Especially for solar panels that don't work when it's cloudy, and wind turbines that don't turn on calm days. Instead, he said, let America be the

OPEC of the future and use our energy power for democracy and human rights.

The legal establishment said that when illegal immigrants come over the border, they are entitled to constitutional rights. But Trump didn't see it that way and asked Mexico to put troops on the frontier to keep them on their side of the border. Mexican president López-Obrador, a hard-line leftist, asked, "Why should we?" But when Trump threatened trade sanctions, López-Obrador saw the light and deployed 28,000 troops. End of problem, and illegal immigration dried up almost entirely.

And to make sure, Trump built five hundred miles of a border wall that everyone was afraid to cross.

The diplomatic establishment had always pushed for the two-state solution in the Middle East. But Trump knew that wouldn't accomplish anything. Hamas would still want to kill Israelis. So he got the United Arab Emirates and Saudi Arabia to stop subsidizing Hamas, in return for our protection against our common enemy—Iran.

The civil rights movement (more specifically, the Black Lives Matter movement) said that minorities have been discriminated against for decades, and that we must abandon the idea of equality. Instead, they claimed that we must begin discriminating against white people. They called it "equity." Trump stood firm for colorblind government and cut the ground out from under them by ushering in policies that led to Black household income rising to historic heights.

He imposed crippling sanctions on Iranian ayatollahs, Russian oligarchs, and Venezuelan dictators.

The president pulled out of the Paris Accord when Europe refused to demand that China stop emitting massive amounts of carbon dioxide into the atmosphere.

Then he defied the environmental lobby by supporting an increase in fracking. As a result, we extracted enough natural gas to cut our carbon emissions by over eight hundred million metric tons—more than Europe and Japan combined.

He alienated the military establishment by demanding withdrawal from the Middle East, even as he wiped out ISIS.

He scrapped NAFTA and negotiated a new deal that stopped China from sneaking products into the United States, and allowed duty free hemispheric trade in autos only for those goods produced by Mexican, American, or Canadian workers who are paid at least $15 per hour—the first and only trade deal in history to incentivize higher wages.

He alienated the legal establishment by appointing Supreme Court justices who uphold our values.

The intelligence "community" hated him for exposing their corrupt lying about his so-called collusion with Russia.

Silicon Valley bristled at his attempts to stop it from controlling and censoring the content that its amazing technology has put at our fingertips. He insisted that media that distributes information electronically could no more censor the news than those that send it out via broadcast or cable. Free speech is free speech, he said.

He paid for his sins with his presidency when the establishments he offended ganged up on him and tried to finish him off.

But his most serious error was to incur the wrath of the media. They hated him as they have never hated any politician, crime boss, dictator, or even mass murderer before. It was a blood lust.

Why? Because he was their rival for power—the only force that could defeat him, and did.

In the beginning, journalists covered the news. Perhaps it was during the Vietnam War that reporters felt that so passive a role was irresponsible. When they realized the extent to which they had been manipulated by Johnson and Nixon—and how they had misled the country by selling the war—they decided, collectively, that they needed to play a more proactive role, not just as journalists, but as investigators—even prosecutors.

Watergate was their revenge. And through a dreary trail of scandals, they confronted politicians and asserted their power. The CIA revelations before the Church Committee, the Iran-Contra scandal, the Clinton scandals, the lack of WMD in Iraq, and the abuse of prisoners at Guantánamo and Abu Ghraib prisons followed in quick succession. Each scandal brought the scalp of a politician or two, and more power to the media. Then came Barack Obama, a political leader who filled the role the media had scripted for him, and he did not disappoint them. He gave the media the total power it craved. What a cold bath Trump was by comparison! Not only did he refuse to toe the line, he reveled in the ensuing confrontation. He labeled the media "fake news," and caught them in a massive lie—with their pants down—in the Russia meddling scandal.

The media had skewered elected presidents before, but never like a paid hit job. Their credibility was under attack, and their power threatened to its core. Trump had to go. For *The New York Times*, *The Washington Post*, *USA Today*, Reuters, ABC, NBC, CBS, CNN, and even *The Wall Street Journal*, it was a matter of survival to bring him down by any means possible.

He had awakened sleeping, and largely trusting, middle America to one central fact: the media does not care what happens to them. They had blocked out the voices of sixty or seventy million voters who were united in their appreciation of, and gratitude toward, Trump. Those people were just too much of a threat. They should stay where they belonged—in fly-over country.

So the establishments—the Democratic Party, the modern-day civil rights movement, Silicon Valley, Big Tech, and parts of Wall Street—ganged up to bring an end to this nightmare.

The media became like *Pravda* or Radio Moscow during the Cold War, blocking news favorable to Trump. And when they had to carry some, they put the most negative spin on it. Good jobs and economic growth data were always conditioned with a dire warning that the next quarter would be terrible. Good news about the environment, Middle East peace, the impact of sanctions on Iran, progress in stopping illegal immigration, and even progress on cutting carbon emissions never appeared in print or on the air.

Realizing that they could not defeat him fairly, they tried everything—preventing him from taking office, impeaching him, and then impeaching him again.

Their success in ultimately replacing him represented their ultimate revenge. Nothing will ever be the same again.

Will Trump Run? Will Trump Win?

Yes and yes!

I have spoken with the former president dozens of times since he left office, and our conversations were always either about how he was cheated in 2020, or how he would get back in in 2024. He has never, for a moment, taken his eye off the ball—getting back in the White House!

Yes, but can he win?

Not only can he win, he *will* win, and nobody else can.

As surely as he was our 45th president, he will be our 47th as well!

Trump's political power is rooted in his unique ability to attract, as no other American political figure can, two key groups of swing voters who became part of his core constituency: white high-school-educated voters and Hispanic-American patriots.

It began in 2016, when Donald Trump discovered a new ethnic group who had lain hidden in our politics, unknown to the oddsmakers, consultants, pundits, and analysts in the news media and the political establishment: the white high-school graduate living in middle America. "Fly-over country," the insiders sneered. The states that don't matter, and the voters who don't really count.

Hillary famously called them the "deplorables." Obama mocked them, saying, "It's not surprising, then, that they get bitter, they cling to guns or religion or antipathy toward people who aren't like them, or anti-immigrant sentiment, or anti-trade sentiment as a way to explain their frustrations."[1]

But Trump understood them, listened to what they had to say, and made them into a political movement that swept the land.

"Poetry is about the grief. Politics is about the grievance,"[2] wrote poet Robert Frost. Donald Trump knew how to translate one into the other.

Low wages, closing factories, shrinking towns, and shattered dreams were the grief that gripped these Americans.

Illegal immigration that dragged down wages and created a class of working poor, ruinous and unfair competition with China, and trade deals that let Mexico steal our jobs—those were the grievances.

And when Trump ripped up NAFTA, sanctioned China, and built a wall along the Southern border—those were the solutions.

In 2020, Trump discovered yet another silent constituency and mobilized them to become a new force in politics—America's Hispanic and Latino patriots.

Overshadowed by the high-profile demands of the African-American community, ignored in the debate over illegal immigration, antagonized in their patriotism by the smears of the woke Left against their adopted country that they had risked their lives to reach, nobody spoke for them, or even much listened.

They had played their assigned role in Jesse Jackson's Rainbow Coalition, but the promised pot of gold at its end always eluded them.

Name some major African-American leaders, past and present. Barack Obama, James Clyburn, John Lewis, Dr. Martin Luther King Jr., Coretta Scott King, Eleanor Holmes Norton, Maxine Waters, General Colin Powell, Justice Clarence Thomas, Senator Tim Scott, Condi Rice, Senator Cory Booker. The list goes on.

Now name the Democratic Hispanic-American leaders. A few names dribble out. Not many. Justice Sotomayor. From the past, Cesar Chavez. Who else?

With almost 19 percent of US population (compared to 14 percent for Blacks), Trump realized that Latinos could become the tail that wagged the dog.

Trump gained eight points among Latino voters between the elections of 2016 and 2020, coming extremely close to carrying them in the key states of Florida and Texas.

It would be both facile and wrong to believe that another American politician would do as well with these two previously neglected constituencies—white high-school graduates, and Latinos.

But beyond the demographics, Trump's brand of straight talk stands out in welcome contrast to the restrained bureaucratic lingo of so many political figures whose speeches sound like diplomatic communiqués, offending nobody and saying less.

To attract white high-school graduates, President Trump skewed his tax cuts to benefit them more than any other demographic group. While Republicans like the Bushes, and even Reagan, focused their tax cuts on reducing the high-income tax brackets, much of Trump's tax reduction came through the $2,000-per-child tax credit passed in 2017, as part of his Tax Cuts and Jobs Act (TCJA). For poor people who paid too little in taxes to use the credit fully, Trump provided $1,400 per child in cash.

The Trump tax cut brought huge relief to working people and reduced the income disparity between rich and poor in the United States dramatically. It was the first tax cut, really, to mean something to the working class.

Equally important for the target group of high-school-educated workers were the trade tariffs Trump imposed on China, vastly reducing the number of closing factories or exported jobs.

Finally, Trump's effective bans on illegal immigration materially raised wages of the American working class.

Despite their exalted rhetoric, Democrats and liberals had largely overlooked the white worker, focusing their attention—and their largesse—on minorities.

Feeling overlooked, overshadowed, and overtaxed, the white working class responded by giving Trump incredibly strong margins of victory in his races against Hillary and Biden.

And here's why: Compare the rise in wages for lower-income workers under Obama with those under Trump.

The bottom 25 percent of earners made a buck and a half more per hour under Obama, a pittance compared with the five dollars more per hour they made under Trump.

U.S. Hourly Wage Growth	
Bottom Quarter	
Hourly wage growth under Obama	$1.48
Hourly wage growth under Trump	$5.14

Source: Bureau of Labor Statistics

But more than the jobs and wages, Trump earned their trust in a way that no other politician ever has. To assume that this trust is transferable to some other candidate would be a serious mistake. There is only one Donald Trump.

5

Donald and Me

O F COURSE, I CAN hardly be an impartial observer where Donald Trump is concerned. I have known him all my life.

My father, Eugene J. Morris, was the top real estate attorney for, first, Fred Trump, and then Donald himself. In his New York City real estate career, a trio of Trump, my father, and political fixer Roy Cohn worked together closely. Trump would handle the financing, Cohn would do the politics, and Dad would be the lawyer. Roy and my father were first cousins, and Roy's first job out of law school was at my Dad's law firm, Demov & Morris.

My father was Trump's lawyer on the development of Trump Tower, the flagship Trump property in Midtown Manhattan.

The president was always generous in his praise of my father, once telling Eileen and me over dinner at his Mar-a-Lago resort in Florida, "Gene Morris was the best real estate lawyer I ever had. He handled Trump Tower for me—the only time I ever really needed a real estate lawyer."

Then, being Trump, he turned to me and said, "He was nothing like you. He wasn't political."

For his part, Roy Cohn was Trump's mentor, guiding him through the maze of New York politics, and many people said, schooling the future president in his tactics of defending himself by ruthlessly attacking his critics.

Roy was known, and in some circles, reviled for prosecuting Julius and Ethel Rosenberg, the famous Russian spies, when he was only twenty-three. When the couple were both executed, the Left raised hell. But subsequent disclosures from secret KGB files have proven that Julius was indeed a spy, and Ethel his enabler.

Then Roy won no popularity with the legal establishment by serving as chief counsel to the Senate committee chaired by Senator Joseph McCarthy in the early 1950s, that investigated alleged Communist infiltration of the State Department, the diplomatic corps, and the US military. Cohn was prominently featured on television, cross-examining witnesses in the widely seen Army-McCarthy hearings and accusing them of being Communist operatives or dupes. McCarthy's and Roy's tactics have entered the lexicon as "McCarthyism."

After McCarthy's ruthless tactics and wild accusations led to his censure by the US Senate, Cohn entered the private practice of law, but not before he was indicted in the early 1960s, three times on federal charges of corruption.

The federal indictments were engineered by the new attorney general, Robert F. Kennedy. Bobby hated Roy because he had lost out when both applied to McCarthy for the job of committee counsel.

Kennedy's revenge led to not one, not two, but three indictments of Cohn. These encounters only served to burnish Roy's reputation for legal brilliance as he eschewed counsel and represented himself as defense attorney, winning three acquittals, disproving the adage that "anyone who represents himself has a fool for a client."

In private practice, Roy was much in demand. His most famous clients were Fred Trump, Donald Trump, and their company; Yankees owner George Steinbrenner; Aristotle Onassis; Rupert Murdoch; mafia figures Tony Salerno, Carmine Galante, and John Gotti; and the Roman Catholic Archdiocese of New York.

A family story about Roy centers around his habit of lunching at the 21 Club, a fashionable restaurant in Manhattan. Even as the restaurant valued his patronage, it was ashamed of him and usually sought to hide him at a table in the back, next to the kitchen.

Roy got his revenge in typical fashion by making a reservation one day for three people for lunch and arriving first. Then, his clients, the Duke and Duchess of Windsor, came to see their attorney, Mr. Cohn. Sheepishly, the maître d' rushed over to offer Roy a "more suitable table." But Cohn was having none of it. "No," he said "this is the table you always put me at, and I'm having lunch here, if you don't mind," he replied. After a luncheon during which waiters had to tiptoe and hold the kitchen doors while making no noise inside, Roy made his point, and henceforth, always got good tables.

Roy's fame spread to the current generation through the 1991 play and film *Angels In America,* about his homosexuality and death from AIDS in 1986. Roy, who was flamboyantly gay, nevertheless stoutly denied his homosexuality, maintaining, in his last illness, that he was suffering from liver cancer, not AIDS. Known for his symbiotic relationship with judges whom he had promoted, Roy, facing death and judgment, asks, "Who's the judge?"

Roy Cohn and my father were very close. My paternal grandfather, a ne'er-do-well, abandoned his family when Gene was only three years old. My Dad, his sister, and his mother moved in with the Cohn family. Gene was a big brother to Roy, who was seventeen years his junior.

My close family ties with President Trump always made me a part of his extended family. We were, in Yiddish words, *mishpocha* (*miss-pop-uh*). Eileen and I first met him and his wife Ivana in the late '70s, when they came to dinner at my parents' apartment. Eileen remembers how Ivana was suffering with a broken leg and had difficulty maneuvering in her cast.

Our political relationship flourished during the 2020 campaign. I had not been active in his first campaign because I suffered from tongue cancer and required two surgeries at Yale New Haven Hospital, and a two-month course of radiation at MD Anderson Cancer Center in Houston, Texas.

During his presidency, I became increasingly enthusiastic as I watched—from my hospital bed—Trump's governing style and achievements.

Having worked for Bill Clinton during his governorship (1978–1992) and his first term as president (1994–1996), it seemed odd to many that I would end up being a fan of Donald Trump.

But there was nothing unusual about it for me. My chief task, when Bill Clinton asked me to help steer his presidency, was to guide him on his journey to the political center after his liberalism during his first two years in office had led to the shipwreck of Republican control of Congress in the Gingrich Revolution. In the late '80s, I had become a Republican, and it was as a Republican that Clinton hired me to help lead him to a bipartisan style of governing. I came to be identified with Clinton's singular achievements of welfare reform and the balanced budget. I called the strategy of defying partisan boundaries by crafting a third way, "triangulation."

So when Trump began to achieve goals that Clinton could only dream of, my work for him was a natural fit.

In April 2020, when I went on board with the Trump campaign, I told the president that "I listened to your State of the Union speech in 2020 and found a remarkable similarity to the speeches I helped draft for Clinton" (that included the famous line, "The era of big government is over."). The big difference, I told President Trump, was that where Clinton could only talk about his hopes and plans to limit illegal immigration by building a border wall, raise wages by middle-class tax cuts, and fight crime with mandatory sentencing, "you spoke of all these things in the past tense, because you had actually succeeded in doing them."

After that initial conversation with the president, I began to phone him regularly, at the beginning every week, and by the summer, pretty much every day. We had ninety-seven phone conversations in all.

We never met in person during the campaign. It was all by telephone. My bout with cancer and my age (seventy-three) left me vulnerable to COVID, so I stayed tucked in my home in Redding, Connecticut. We did not see one another in person until June 2021, when he graciously invited me to join him as he golfed at his Briarcliff Manor resort in Westchester County, New York (see the cover photo).

Golfing with Trump is really an exercise in track and field. He races through the course like a runner pursuing Olympic gold, gunning his golf cart from green to green. He owns the course, so I guess for him, there's no speed limit.

I don't golf, but it was exhausting enough watching him.

He's actually a damn good golfer. The pro who accompanied us said he had worked with six former presidents, and that Trump was the best. His drives were robust, fast, and usually straight down the fairway. His putting was patient and well-aimed.

At one hole, however, he hit his ball into a water trap, a small pond. "Part the waters, Mister President," I advised after the splash.

Knowing that I don't golf, Eileen was surprised when the president told her, "Dick knows all about golf." She replied, "He must have read a book."

When the president described the outing to a mutual friend, he was even more graphic, saying, "That Dick Morris, he really knows a lot about golf!" Trump then explained how he had discovered my expertise. "He says I'm a great golfer!" Typical Trump.

John McLaughlin, my longtime colleague and friend, was my close collaborator in working on the campaign. John had served as Trump's pollster in the 2016 election. I had originally introduced him to Trump in 2008, as Trump explored a possible race for president. I delivered a series of issue briefings to the future president, and asked John to accompany me to the meetings.

John is the best pollster in America. (He might be the only good one.) He is free from the leftist bias of most establishment polls, and his data is incredibly accurate. One of the top consultants, whom I used in the Clinton campaign of '96, the late Bob Squier, once said that getting data from most pollsters was akin to drawing it from a vending machine—no analysis, no interpretation. President Clinton, who fired his pollster, Stan Greenberg, after I went back into his orbit at the White House, complained that Stan, like so many other pollsters, "never told me what to do." It was always "on the one hand . . . on the other hand . . . "

That wasn't John's style, or mine. So we were a natural fit, using polls to shape our political messaging. We would take Trump's well-formulated positions on key issues and regard them as a menu from which to order that day's message. With a candidate like Trump, you can't tell him what to say. But you often need to guide him on when to say it and how to phrase it. While working closely with Stephen Miller, Trump's best speechwriter, that's what John and I tried to do.

Our involvement in the campaign kicked into high gear after my sojourn at MD Anderson Hospital in Houston. Eileen and I decided to use the extra time we had been granted to help Trump get re-elected.

On Friday, April 24, 2020, we called the president directly and spoke with him for almost an hour. It was the first of nearly a hundred phone calls—several each week—with the president over the rest of the year.

We refused any payment. Some said that Trump was suspicious of those he paid, worried that he was being ripped off. We felt that by turning down any formal role in the campaign, we could skirt the infighting that raged inside.

We also decided, jointly with the president, that the calls and our consulting role should be kept secret. And so it remained for the ensuing seven months.

Only campaign chief Jared Kushner; White House Chief of Staff Mark Meadows; pollster John McLaughlin; speechwriter Stephen Miller; scheduler Hope Hicks; the president's personal assistant, Molly Michaels; media creator Larry Weitzner; and campaign staffers Brad Pascale, Jason Miller, and Bill Stepien knew of our involvement.

But John McLaughlin was our chief partner. John shared all of the president's polling data—at his request—with us and guided us through the labyrinth that was the Trump campaign. John worked closely with us in refining strategic thinking, war gaming the election, and handling the often resentful campaign staff.

But apart from those ten people, our work with the president was a closely guarded secret.

President Trump liked it that way.

But some of those privy to the secret didn't like it very much. The regular campaign staff—primarily Bill Stepien and Jason Miller—wanted to control the flow of poll data to the president. Hard to steer in the best of times, they feared that Trump would veer totally out of control if the data was bad. In one poll, McLaughlin found that Trump had fallen dramatically. Stepien and Miller tried to keep the data from the president, and specifically passed the message to me not to tell him. I never, ever believe in concealing poll data from the client, and told the president, "Stepien and Miller don't want me to share the polling data with you." Then I asked, "What do you want me to do?" The president, as expected, told me to share the data, but then, unexpectedly, told me not to tell Stepien or Miller I was doing so. McLaughlin got the same answer. In reply, Jason Miller sent out a text that nobody was to share any polling data with me. The president told John and me to ignore the instruction.

Indeed, after that experience, neither Stepien nor Jason Miller, nor even Jared, would allow McLaughlin to poll again, likely for fear that he would tell the president. They said it was because the campaign was financially strapped. I told Jared that this was like shutting off a plane's radar to save electricity. "The only pilots that don't use radar are kamikazes," I quipped.

But John and I managed to secure reliable polling data from which to advise the president working with John Jordan, a brilliant political advisor.

Typically, Eileen and I would contact the president by phoning the White House switchboard. The phone number—(202) 456-1414—had been emblazoned on my memory from my days of close contact with President Bill Clinton from 1994 through 1996. President Trump put us on a list of people who could be put through to him directly. Most of the time, he wasn't available and would call back.

Curiously, when he returned our call—usually fairly quickly— our iPhone would indicate that the call was coming from Egypt, and that it was a spam risk. When we answered, one of the White House operators came on the line. We got to know them and sometimes even chatted briefly.

There is no thrill quite like the one you feel when the operator comes back and says, "The president will speak with you now." An adrenaline rush! Get ready! Organize your thoughts! Then the familiar voice would come on: "Hi, Dick. Hi, Eileen. What's up? How am I doing?"

We usually spoke with the president by speakerphone, with both of us on the line. We felt that the president treated us warmly, almost as members of his extended family. On saying goodbye, he would usually say, "So long, kids."

Once, I read him a draft ad attacking the Democrats for urging the defunding of the police. You may have seen it. The ad showed an empty police station where the phone kept ringing in vain. Then the tape on the phone said: "You have reached the emergency number at the police department. Due to budget cuts, there's nobody here to answer your call. Please press one to report a rape, two to report a murder, and three for a home invasion. For all other matters, please leave your name, address, and phone number. Average wait time is five days." The president loved it. "That's great!" he said. "Send it to Molly [his exec assistant Molly Michael]. Get it on the air right away!" Then came the playful dig. "You didn't write that," he said flatly. "I know who wrote it. Eileen wrote it. You have the genes (referring to my father), but she has the brains."

To summarize months of advice, I believe that Eileen, John, and I contributed three key insights to the campaign.

The first was what we called the Frank Perdue Theory. Perdue was a regular fixture on television in the northeast in the '80s and '90s, as he hawked his chickens under the slogan, "It takes a tough man to make a tender chicken." The slogan stuck with me. Could we apply it to Trump?

In our polling, John and I found that half the voters who didn't like Trump disliked his "temperament and personality," but agreed with his "programs and positions." There was not much that we could do about his policies, but could we rein in his temperament and personality?

Lots of luck with that one!

Trump is Trump. Like it or lump it. He'll never change, and I came to realize that his manner could not be divorced from his successful outcomes. Change one, and you would forfeit the other.

So we looked to Frank Perdue for guidance. If he could persuade America that it took a tough man to make a tender chicken, perhaps we could make the point that it took one to make a good president.

We urged the Trump campaign to say, in effect, "It's OK to support Trump, even if you don't like his style, because of the great record he has amassed." And further, "It takes a Donald Trump to change Washington." Sometimes we related the Frank Perdue strategy to voters' dislike of the "swamp" in Washington by saying, "This is what Washington has come to . . . it takes a Donald Trump to get things done." The president and his son-in-law, Jared Kushner, both liked the strategy. They felt that it was the missing link in selling Donald Trump to the voters.

The Frank Perdue strategy even made its way into a Trump ad that aired during the 2019 World Series, written by Eileen and produced by media consultant Larry Weitzner. It said that the president "is no Mr. Nice Guy, but sometimes it takes a Donald Trump to change Washington." We were giving the voters permission—and a rationale—to dislike Trump but to still vote for him.

Our second suggestion came after Kushner called me just as Trump had taken to the road to host his first rally of the year on June 20th in Tulsa, Oklahoma. He complained that the campaign lacked a coherent theme in its attacks on Biden. "We have Hunter Biden's corruption, Joe Biden's flip-flops on key issues as he tried to erase his less-than-liberal record in the Senate, and the increasing evidence of his dementia and senility." Jared said, "But it's all over the place. We have to pull it together into one theme."[1]

In a nap right after Jared's call, I dreamed the answer.

I woke with a start and frantically tried to put my dream ideas down in a text to Jared, afraid that I might forget them.

That text was the forerunner of our eventual strategy.

I looked at the spectacle of the radical Left, and at the world they would create in America if we gave them the chance. As I thought about it, it seemed like a society right out of Ayn Rand's dystopian narrative *Atlas Shrugged* (a book I had just recently finally gotten around to reading, at the suggestion of Mark Levin).

As fast as my thumbs could move, I banged out a text to Jared. (I touch type rapidly, but in texting, I am a clumsy, all-thumbs guy.)

"I've got it!" the screed began. "Biden is so weak, so senile, the crazies on the Left will take over. No police. No cars. No free speech. Crime runs rampant. Open borders. Terrorists and druggies flood in. All drugs legalized. Huge taxes. Everything is determined by affirmative action. No standards for doctors or professionals. Anybody gets in. Mass government medicine. Not enough doctors. Medicare swamped. Political correctness reigns. Climate change deniers guilty of a crime. Locked up. Criminals go free. Anti-Semitism. Anti-Israel. Biden is like von Hindenburg was in Weimar [Germany]. Incapable of controlling Hitler. Biden is incapable of controlling AOC or Pelosi. So weak that he becomes Pelosi's puppet, and she, in turn, is run by the likes of AOC."

"Everyone knows the Left is nuts, and Biden is weak, so put them together: No coal. No oil. No fracking. Permissive schools. Anything goes. Washington Monument and Jefferson Memorial renamed. They had slaves. Reparations."

"And Biden can't deny it without pissing off his base. His convention becomes a brawl as progressives try to get their platform."

"Trump is safe and sane by comparison."

"Campus becomes a no-go zone. Lefties control corporate boards. People flee cities. Unsafe. Voting age to sixteen. No registration. No IDs. Anyone votes. George Soros's America lives. No free press. Left takes over media. Fires any writer or editor who doesn't toe the line. Wealth tax. Ten percent haircut every year."

Then I moved to a critique of our current slogan. ("Biden: Too wrong for too long.")

"'Too wrong for too long' is wrong theme. Implies that Biden is safe, predictable. That he is a known quantity with all his flaws. Not so bad. Key is to highlight the unknown new danger when the progressives jerk his chain and take over his presidency."

Jared was enthusiastic, and the next day, as I read the text to the president, it was clear that we had our issue.

Stephen Miller, Trump's incredible speech writer, hammered out the message in a speech for the Tulsa rally. Excitedly, we watched as the president unveiled his new issue. It wasn't that Biden was too liberal. It was that his age and appearance of dementia had made him too weak to resist the leftward lurch of his own party.

With twelve thousand cheering Trump supporters in attendance, the president outlined his main campaign themes, some drawn from my text, But the media paid no attention. They were only interested in covering the virus. Nothing the president said mattered. Their stories focused instead on the president's failure to wear a mask or to insist that those attending the event put one on, too.

Because the media warned people not to risk attending the rally, many Trump voters chose to stay home instead. The Tulsa auditorium was only half-full. The empty seats stood out on the television cameras. Wasn't Tulsa supposed to be Trump land?

When former presidential candidate Herman Cain died shortly after attending the rally and contracting the virus, the media used it to hype the hysteria. (Herman, with whom I worked in 2012, was a great man and one of my heroes.)

Suddenly, all that mattered was that the president had not been masked. Masks and the virus took over the entire campaign—just what Pelosi wanted.

I battled hard—with less success—to persuade the president to wear a mask.

Eileen, John, and I worried that his refusal to wear a mask fed Biden's charge that the president didn't get it—that the virus was a true national emergency. By attacking Trump for not wearing a mask, the Democrats were covering for their candidate, who was too senile and clueless to campaign much in person. Always wearing a big black mask in public, Biden seemed to be wearing a muzzle to stop him from speaking or committing gaffes that brought into question his mental ability.

I pressed the president hard to wear a mask. I even asked Jared to help. His reply was clear: On this one, you're on your own. The day after the president's July 4th rally, I put it bluntly: "All that stands between you and a second term is a damned piece of cloth. Biden's entire campaign is that he wears a mask, and you don't."

The president pleaded that he had nothing against masks, but still cited the fact that several people he knew wore masks but still got the virus. I became increasingly heated—something you could do with Trump, unlike most presidents—and said, "Sir, you have a choice: get defeated, or wear the damn mask. Wear the fucking mask!" I exploded into the phone. "If you just put the thing on, you take away the only issue Biden has."

Perhaps surprised at my ferocity, the president lamely asked, "Do I have to wear it all the time? Even when I'm speaking?"

"Walk up to the mike with your mask on, and then ostentatiously remove it to give your speech," I replied.

"I'm going to visit Walter Reed [hospital] over the weekend. I'll wear a mask," he promised.

When Eileen and I saw the president wearing a mask for the first time in public, we celebrated and toasted glasses.

How stupid Biden seemed! Campaigning on a virus that we thought was going away! Jared, who the president had designated to be in charge of fighting COVID, assured me that the virus would begin to fade "in three weeks" (by the end of July). Indeed, the statistics justified our complacency. New virus cases did drop appreciably as the election approached, from seventy thousand a day, down to only twenty-five thousand per day in early September. We did not realize, at the time, that the case count would then mount every day thereafter, reaching ninety-three thousand by Election Day.[2]

We took comfort in knowing that daily deaths stayed low, dropping to three hundred in early September, before gradually rising to over one thousand on Election Day.

Earlier, it had seemed that Biden's emphasis on the virus had fallen short, and our focus on rebuilding the economy in its wake was hitting home. From the start of the virus, all polls showed that while voters—by eight points—trusted Biden more than Trump to fight the virus, they trusted Trump more—also by ten points—to rebuild the economy. So it seemed to us that Biden was fighting for the past—to control the virus—while we were battling for the future—rebuilding afterward.

But all along, Biden was playing the Republicans for fools by hyping concerns about the virus. We all assumed that Biden's objective in focusing on COVID was to win votes by talking about his best issue: who would be better on the virus.

But we missed that this was not really his point at all. He wanted to drive fear of the virus so that voters would stay home and vote by mail or absentee ballot. While the Trump campaign honchos were patting themselves on the back for our climbing poll numbers, Biden's people were happily watching as tens of millions of ballots arrived by mail, largely from Democrats. Was his plan all along to encourage mail-in voting to permit shenanigans?

Our third point of focus came during October, a month before the election. John and I noticed in our polling how Latinos were voting for Trump in unusually heavy numbers.

At the time, the main campaign focused on the Black vote, tending to ignore Hispanics. But John and I felt that while Trump deserved to get more Black votes, and would likely do so, our really fertile ground was among Hispanics. Even so, while Trump did gain three points among African Americans, he soared by ten among Latinos. Specifically, our polls showed that Hispanics, many of them recent arrivals, were antagonized by the virulence with which the Left denounced America, a country many of them had risked their lives to reach.

In my phone calls with the president, I emphasized our enormous gains among Latinos. Many urged Trump to adopt a softer line on immigration to win more Hispanics, but John and I had closely examined the motivation of the Hispanic vote years earlier, when we polled Latinos in partnership with John Jordan, a good friend and a conservative political pundit from the California wine country. Jordan theorized that it was not through the immigration issue, but through patriotism and nationalism, that we could bring Latinos into our ranks.

McLaughlin and I tested Jordan's insight and found it to be spot on. While Democrats were, symbolically, seeing Hispanics as still at the border, obsessed with immigration, Jordan realized that they had largely left the border far behind in their own, or their ancestors', past, and were now looking at it from afar, as other Americans do.

In Jordan's poll, Latinos cited education, jobs, and health care as their top issues, with immigration reform a distant fourth.

When the BLM and Antifa demonstrations started in the wake of George Floyd's murder, McLaughlin and I consulted with Jordan and did another round of survey research. We concluded that Hispanics were deeply offended to hear their adopted country derided and insulted as racist and exploitive.

Jordan's work opened our eyes to another salient fact about Hispanics that the Democrats had missed: There was a sharp difference in the importance of the immigration issue between those Latinos who were born here, and those who had come as immigrants. Or in the case of Puerto Ricans, as migrants.

There was about a twenty-point gap between them. Foreign-born immigrants (one-third of Latino voters), resented restrictions on illegal immigration and tended to view them as anti-Hispanic. But the other two-thirds, those who were born in the United States, saw it much as other Americans did: an influx of uninvited and illegal immigrants who would compete with them for jobs and housing.

Democratic strategists completely missed this fault line in the Latino community. That's partially because the special interest groups that plead the case for illegal immigration are largely led by immigrants themselves who have not fully adopted the mindset of native-born Americans on this issue.

The LULAC (League of United Latin American Citizens) is a radical leftist group that closely follows the Democratic Party line, endorsing its candidates and echoing its views. As such, it is out of touch with the views of many Hispanic voters, and missed the key point: that abusing America is a massive turnoff for Latino voters, and coddling those who attack our country will curry no favor with Hispanic Americans.

Led by the nose by LULAC, the Democrats missed the point that Jordan made, and the oversight led to their losses among Hispanics in 2020.

Jordan had the opportunity to relate his findings directly to President Trump in an October phone call that lasted half an hour. Trump got the message, and in subsequent weeks, pounded the extreme Left's attack on our history and values, with an eye to the Hispanic vote.

In following Jordan's strategy, Trump laid the basis for a permanent realignment of the Latino vote. As long as the Democrats put down America and topple our statues, they will continue to alienate Hispanics and Asians who came to this country because they believed in it . . . and in us!

6

A Kinder, Gentler Trump?

A LOT OF PEOPLE COME up to me and say, "Trump is his own worst enemy." They mean that they largely approve of his direction and policies, but that his constant battles with the media, Congress, and many of the leaders of his own party are a turnoff.

"Why can't he just modulate his style—be nicer and less confrontational?" they ask, echoing our poll finding that a quarter of the voters like his "programs and positions," but not his "personality and temperament."

These folks don't get it—that his temperament and accomplishments are cause and effect. If you modulate the temperament, you won't get the accomplishments.

Like it or not, Trump governed by intimidation. He got his way with his own party, Congress, foreign leaders, and even the media by threats, loud complaints, accusations, and bullying. In 2016, Trump did not so much win the GOP nomination as orchestrate a hostile takeover of the party. Not a pretty picture, but an effective way to govern.

Intimidating His Own Party

How did Donald Trump, a political novice, manage to keep his own party in line and pass his conservative agenda with the nearly unanimous Republican support he needed in the closely divided Congress?

He did it by scaring the hell out of his senators. The best examples are the public executions of renegade Republican Senators Bob Corker of Tennessee and Jeff Flake of Arizona.

Both men defied Trump, and both paid for it with their political careers.

In January 2018, Senator Flake unloaded on Trump, calling the president's criticism of the media an "assault as unprecedented as it is unwarranted." He particularly objected to Trump's accusation that the media was an "enemy of the people," a charge first made by Soviet dictator Josef Stalin against dissidents in his own Communist Party. "It is a testament," he said, "to the condition of our democracy that our own president uses words infamously spoken by Joseph Stalin to describe his enemies," Flake said, noting that Stalin used the charge to "annihilate such individuals who disagreed with the supreme leader."[1]

Flake also criticized Trump's tax cuts, which led the president to declare his political career "toast," and to affix a nickname to the senator: "Jeff Flake(y)."[2]

Flake retired from the Senate in 2018, and endorsed Biden in 2020.

Also in the president's crosshairs was Tennessee Senator Bob Corker, chairman of the Senate Foreign Relations Committee. Corker endorsed Obama's nuclear agreement with Iran, jimmying the rules so it did not need two-thirds approval in the Senate for ratification (as the Constitution requires), but only needed one-third of the vote to validate it. (When Congress passed a bill blocking the treaty, Obama vetoed it and then needed only one-third to sustain his veto).

Corker attacked Trump's overtures to North Korea, saying that they brought us closer to war. He mocked Trump, saying, "It's a shame the White House has become an adult day care center. Someone obviously missed their shift this morning."[3]

Trump replied that Corker had "helped President Obama give us the bad Iran deal, and couldn't get elected dog catcher in Tennessee."[4]

After the election of 2018—when Corker didn't run—he was gone.

There remained, however, two ghosts who regularly attended the Republican caucus in the Senate—Corker and Flake—to remind everyone what happens when you cross Donald Trump.

Intimidating Foreign Leaders

Trump's success in foreign policy was largely based on threats and intimidation against Russia, China, Iran, Venezuela, Cuba, and even our NATO allies. The flipside of the coin, of course, was North Korea, where a charm offensive, after initial threats, proved effective.

It is said that Richard Nixon maintained that the president of the United States must make clear to the chairman of the Council of Ministers of the Union of Soviet Socialist Republics that he's "nuts." Nuts enough to drop the bomb.

That's just what Trump did to Kim Jong-un, the North Korean dictator. Kim began the exchange by bragging that he had a nuclear button he could push to punish the United States for its attacks on his country. Trump replied that he had a "bigger button" than Kim did.[5]

After that, it was smooth sailing between the two leaders. After a series of summit meetings, they reached something of a détente. While there was no overt agreement, North Korea refrained from nuclear weapons tests or ballistic missile firings for the remaining three years of the Trump presidency (but then resumed them immediately after Biden took office).

Trump drew extensive criticism when he publicly attacked our NATO allies during a summit meeting of its leaders in 2017. He blasted them for their minimal contribution to NATO's military, saying, "I have been very, very direct . . . in saying that NATO members must finally contribute their fair share."[6]

It worked. On November 29, 2019, NATO Secretary General Jens Stoltenberg announced that "in 2019, defense spending across European allies and Canada increased in real terms by 4.6 percent, making this the fifth consecutive year of growth." He also revealed that by the end of 2020, those allies will have invested $130 billion more since 2016. He said, "This is unprecedented progress, and it is making NATO stronger."[7]

Trump's aggressive posture likely also induced China not to complain too loudly about his tariff increase. It may have also influenced Russia's decision to withdraw its troops from the

Ukraine border, particularly when Trump began to send weapons to Kiev.

To appreciate the magnitude of his policy success, just look at what happened the minute he left office: Russia put troops back on Ukraine border and beefed up its presence in the Arctic. China overflew Taiwan airspace and made threatening moves in the South China Sea. North Korea resumed missile overflights of Japan. ISIS resurfaced and the Taliban went berserk when Biden pulled out of Afghanistan.

If Trump were kinder and gentler, America's enemies would never have been so brazen.

Intimidating the News Media

In Spanish bullfights, picadors come out and stick swords and spears and needles into the bull to enrage him and goad him into fighting. In Washington, DC, we call this process a press conference.

Trump handled the news media like it was an opposing political candidate, hammering at it with negative attacks. His goal was not to change their poll numbers, as he would have done with a political opponent, but to damage the one thing that mattered to their corporate overlords: their ratings. Having extensive experience in the world of television, Trump knew that the advertising revenues of the news stations were directly tied to their ratings, so he mocked their shows as featuring "fake news."

We all know the results of the 2020 election (sort of), but less well-known is that the television networks and cable news shows took a horrible drubbing from which they have still not recovered. Nielsen Media Research ratings showed that CNN was the clear loser of the election of 2020. The network "lost nearly half of its viewers in just one year as major cable news networks struggled in ratings."[8]

- In June 2021, CNN had an average of 580,000 total daily viewers—a drop of 49 percent.
- MSNBC suffered the second-largest drop in viewership and lost 37 percent of its total audience.
- Fox News lost 35 percent of its total viewers after it reported, prematurely, that Trump had lost Arizona on election night.[9]

Meanwhile, Newsmax—ever loyal to Trump—surged. The network's viewer base rose from about 25,000 in the summer of 2020, to 400,000 after the election.

Would a kinder, gentler Trump be as effective? To paraphrase Shakespeare, Would a rose by any other name smell as sweet? Probably not.

7

The Midterms and
the White House

BEFORE WE EVEN GET to 2024, we have to retake Congress in 2022.

Things are looking good.

In twenty-one midterm elections since 1934, the president's party lost ground in Congress in nineteen of them.

The sole exceptions were 1998, when the Republicans lost seats amid national disgust over their obsession with Bill Clinton's affair with Monica Lewinsky, and in 2002, when the country rallied around George W. Bush in the immediate aftermath of 9/11.

So the odds are in our favor.

While the Democrats won the presidency in 2020, they lost ten seats in Congress, cutting their margin of control from thirty-nine seats to only nine. Since the president's party loses an average of thirty seats in midterm elections, Nancy Pelosi's days as Speaker of the House may be numbered.

But beyond the historical trends, this Congress has dismal poll ratings.

At the end of June of 2021, 71 percent of voters disapproved of the job Congress was doing—a big falloff from the 61 percent who had disapproved in March of 2021.

Also encouraging for Republicans:

- Democrats were elected or re-elected from districts Trump carried in 2020.
- Thirteen Democrats and nine Republican House members have announced their retirements for the 2022 cycle, as of October 18, 2021. Four of the five Democratic departures come from Republican-leaning districts likely to flip in 2022. Only one of the retiring Republicans comes from a district we might lose.

With a flip of five seats being enough to transfer control of the House, these trends are favorable.

Never has there been a Congress that has more frequently or more flagrantly ignored public opinion in its votes.

The measures that have passed have been bad enough. With the huge spending bills, and likely, the enormous tax hikes that are to come, the Democratic House and Senate richly deserve their negative ratings.

But in the House, where the Democrats rule with Pelosi's iron hand, the one-House bills they have passed—that were doomed in the Senate—are even worse. Yet incumbent Democratic congressmen have loyally followed their leader and walked off a cliff to back crazy legislation.

Consider what the House Democrats voted for, usually unanimously:

- To force most sole proprietorships to close down and merge into large, unionized corporate structures.
- To prohibit photo-identification requirements for voting and registering.
- To override right-to-work laws in twenty-six states, forcing workers to join unions on pain of losing their jobs.
- To allow trans women to compete against—and inevitably defeat—girls in scholastic sports, often costing the biological women possible college scholarships.
- To offer farm aid, COVID economic relief, and mortgage assistance to "people of color" but not to white people.
- Allow federal Medicaid funds to be used for transgender surgery.

With votes like these, it is a mystery why the Democrats think they can win. My artist friend, Doug DePierro, said it best: "The Democrats are lending credibility to stupidity." Indeed.

And then there is a game changer. In a recent Supreme Court decision, *Rucho v. Common Cause*, the Court, under the leadership of Chief Justice Roberts, decided that it would no longer act as the umpire in redistricting cases. Until then, the Court had always held that it was its duty to make sure that congressional district lines were fair and not subject to gerrymandering. But now, things have changed. The Roberts Court says that it will no longer adjudicate reapportionment cases to reverse instances of partisan gerrymandering. It would still intervene if there were racial gerrymandering, but other than that, the parties are on their own.

Since Republicans control the governorship and both Houses of state legislatures in thirty states, including most of the swing states, this decision creates a field day for the party. Liberals estimate that the partisan reapportionment could cost them as many as thirteen House seats.

Will the Election Be Honest?

There are grounds for optimism, but the situation keeps changing every day.

Here's the state of play: The Democrats caught us napping in 2020, sneaking up to win secretary of state races in Arizona and Michigan so that control of the electoral process would be in the hands of dedicated and ruthless partisans with no regard for integrity. They won't catch us napping again. Republicans have, hopefully, learned that the races of 2022 for secretary of state—in Arizona, Michigan, Wisconsin, and Georgia—will do much to determine who will win in 2024.

Pelosi and Schumer tried to sneak one over on Republicans by introducing HR 1 and S 1, while proclaiming that they were designed to ensure voting rights for minorities. But it became evident that these dangerous bills simply ratified practices that the Democrats used to prevail in 2020.

After the refusal of Senators Joe Manchin (D-WV) and Krysten Sinema (D-AZ) to suspend the filibuster rule to let the Democrats jam these bills through on a party-line vote, it appeared that both bills were unlikely to pass.

Then the Supreme Court stepped in—finally—and upheld the rights of states to exercise their constitutional right to regulate elections. The issue concerned ballot harvesting, but it opened the doors to a plethora of state laws requiring photo

IDs to register or vote, verification of signatures on mail-in and absentee ballots, identification on paper ballots (such as the last four digits of the Social Security number), and bans on "curing" paper ballots.

With forty-one states having passed over a hundred election-integrity bills, the chances of a fair and honest election are increasingly likely.

And How About the Senate?

Calling the probable outcome in the Senate is harder. It boils down to the dynamics of each individual race, and those are hard to determine this far in advance.

The board starts out tilting heavily in the Democrats' direction, but don't lose heart. With the generous—but inadvertent—assistance of a senile, incompetent, arrogant, demented president, we might just pull it off.

There are twenty Republican, but only fourteen Democratic, Senate seats up in 2022.

Five of the GOP incumbents are likely to retire, while all but one of the Democrats are expected to run again—a huge edge for the Democrats because incumbents usually win.

Republican incumbent Senators Richard Burr (NC), Pat Toomey (PA), Richard Shelby (ALA), Rob Portman (OH), and Roy Blunt (MO) are definitely not running in 2022. Shelby's Alabama seat is safe for Republicans, and the GOP should win in the race to succeed Portman in Ohio and Blunt in Missouri. The trouble is that our chances of succeeding Toomey in Pennsylvania and Burr in North Carolina are 50/50. But as Biden's ratings continue to drop, victories there are quite possible, even probable.

Then there are three other Republican Senators who have not decided yet whether they will run for re-election

Republicans were relieved when the eighty-one-year-old Republican Senator from Iowa, Chuck Grassley, announced he is running again, but there are still two other Republican Senators who have not decided yet whether they will run for re-election: Ron Johnson of Wisconsin and John Thune of South Dakota. Thune's seat will go to a Republican regardless of his decision. But Ron Johnson's could still go Democrat whether he runs or not.

On the other hand, four Democratic Senators, all seeking re-election, are in trouble.

Mark Kelly of Arizona, the former astronaut whose Senate bid was aided by sympathy after his wife, Congresswoman Gabrielle Giffords, was shot in 2012. Kelly took her seat when she could not run due to traumatic brain damage. But even then, he won by only 2.4 percent. Since then, he has voted the party line in the Senate, setting him far apart from his colleague, Krysten Sinema, also a Democrat, who has carved out an independent reputation. Kelly doesn't look good by comparison.

Raphael Warnock, the ultra-crazy leftist Senator elected in the hotly disputed Georgia runoff in 2021. He "won" by only 2.1 percent, and should be beatable now that Georgia has closed many of the loopholes that allowed Warnock to win in 2020. And Warnock's opponent is football star Hershel Walker. Count that as a probably GOP pickup.

Also on the chopping block is Democratic incumbent Senator Maggie Hassan of New Hampshire, who narrowly won by only 0.1 percent (one-tenth of one percent) in a cliff-hanger last time.

And Republicans have a shot at knocking off first-term Democratic Senator from Nevada, Catherine Cortez-Masto. But Nevada elections are notoriously dishonest, and I wouldn't bet on the outcome.

So despite heavy odds in the Senate, if there is a red wave in 2022, it should sweep us into Senate control.

Will Harris Be the President or the Democratic Candidate in 2024?

It is far from certain that Biden will be the Democratic candidate in 2024. In fact, he may not last even that long.

I believe that the Democrats nominated Biden, knowing full well that he might not serve out his term, and that this expectation played a role in their decision to endorse him.

Remember the history. Biden limped through the first three Democratic primaries of 2020.

He got only 14 percent of the vote in Iowa, behind Bernie Sanders (27 percent), Pete Buttigieg (25 percent), and Elizabeth Warren (20 percent).

He did worse in New Hampshire, finishing fifth with only 8 percent of the vote, behind Sanders (26 percent), Warren (24 percent), Buttigieg (24 percent), Klobuchar (20 percent), and Warren (9 percent).

It was only in Nevada that he managed a decent showing, placing second after Sanders.

As the field entered the South Carolina primary, South Bend, Indiana mayor Pete Buttigieg had the clear momentum.

South Carolina was Biden's stopper. Since it was the only state primary with a majority African-American vote, the party honchos had scheduled the primary three days before Super Tuesday, when most of the Southern states, with their large Black populations, voted. The idea was that the Black community throughout the South would take their cue from South Carolina.

To win South Carolina, Biden needed the endorsement of Democratic African-American congressman James Clyburn. And sure enough, Clyburn came through, backing Biden a few days before the primary. Biden swept to an impressive win in South Carolina (49 percent of the vote), propelled by Clyburn's Black voters.

Biden swept to victory on Super Tuesday and secured the nomination. A few days later, he announced that he would name a woman as his vice presidential running mate.

That's the record. Now, for rumors and my conjecture.

The rumor has circulated, from reliable insider sources, that Clyburn made Biden promise to name a Black woman as his VP.

And the rumor is that Clyburn had one in mind: Michelle Obama. A close ally of President Obama, the South Carolina congressman may have wanted to lay the basis for a third Obama term, either in the expectation of Biden's death, or incapacity, or of Michelle Obama's winning on her own in 2024.

Either way, it is clear that the Black congressman and party leaders wanted to get their hands back on the Oval Office.

Did Clyburn and the other Black leaders rescue Biden from oblivion because he was so frail, and obviously deteriorating, that he posed no threat to a Black nominee in 2024, or might possibly be unable to serve out his term under the provisions of the Twenty-fifth Amendment to the Constitution?

That Amendment makes a coup d'état by the vice president a distinct possibility. If the VP finds that the president is no longer capable of doing his duty, she can make a declaration to that effect, and if a majority of the Cabinet agrees, become acting president, even if the president is unwilling to co-operate. Then the Amendment provides that the matter goes to the Congress for adjudication. If a two-thirds majority of each House decides that the president is no longer capable, he's out, and the VP is in.

Could the Democrats, led by the Black Caucus, be planning such a move?

Is that why Biden has been so willing to follow their lead?

Lately, a thinly disguised war of leaks has broken out in the Biden-Harris White House, aimed at discrediting the vice president.

On June 30, 2021, *Politico*, a fount of information about the inside workings of the White House under Democratic rule, ran a story headlined: "Not a healthy environment: Kamala Harris' office rife with dissent."[1]

The story, a typical Washington hatchet job, reported that "Harris's team is experiencing low morale, porous lines of communication and diminished trust among aides and senior officials."[2]

The article went on to say that "in interviews, 22 current and former vice-presidential aides, administration officials and associates of Harris and Biden described a tense and at times dour office atmosphere, an insular environment where ideas are ignored or met with harsh dismissals, and decisions are dragged out. Often, they said, [Harris] refuses to take responsibility for delicate issues and blames staffers for the negative results that ensue."[3]

Hit pieces like this always have a source and a purpose in our nation's capital.

The source, cloaked in anonymity, could only have been inside the executive offices of the White House, but it was probably not one of Harris's people. Why would they savage their own boss, their meal ticket?

Most likely, the story was from Biden's people. But why would he dump on Harris? Would the Twenty-fifth Amendment have something to do with it? A fear that she might invoke it as the plain evidence of Biden's incapacity and senility becomes too blatant to ignore?

Remember in 1968, when Nixon chose Spiro Agnew to run as his vice president? People wondered why he had picked a man under serious criminal investigation. When the evidence of his dishonesty came out, and he had to be removed, people speculated that Nixon may have chosen him as a form of insurance. Suspicious of Washington elites, and perhaps fearful of impeachment, did Nixon choose Agnew so that he would have a vice president who couldn't succeed him? In fact, before Nixon could be impeached, insiders exposed Agnew's corruption and ousted him from office, replacing him with the more acceptable Gerald Ford.

Could Biden's people be attacking Harris, portraying her as an unreliable flake, so that Democrats are loath to vote their boss out of office under the Twenty-fifth Amendment?

So how would Harris fare against Trump?

Current evidence, perhaps caused by the covert anti-Harris campaign by Biden operatives, suggests that she would be an even weaker candidate than Biden. Polls generally have her about six points below Biden in general election match ups.

The most recent polls put Biden's job approval in the mid-thirties and Harris' ten points lower.

Remember that she was the early and clear loser of the Democratic primaries of 2020. Her presidential candidacy lasted from January 21, 2019, when she announced her run, until December 3rd of that same year, when she pulled out, driven by bad poll numbers. She never even made it to the first primaries and caucuses.

But Could Someone Else Run . . . Like AOC?

Fasten your seat belts and take a trip with me now into the *Twilight Zone*, into fantasy, into science fiction.

What if the new ultra-Left "progressives" put up a candidate of their own? What if it's Alexandria Ocasio-Cortez (AOC), the young Congresswoman from New York?

Could the "squad" see Donald Trump coming back, likely to win the Republican nomination? What if they look at the spectacle of an old, worn-out, discredited, low-energy, senile Joe Biden and wondered if he could ever stand up to a juggernaut like Trump?

It's easy to see AOC raising the flag to rally the left behind a more energetic, charismatic, younger candidate . . . and a female Hispanic, to boot.

It could happen gradually. She could evolve into the role.

First, she is now watching Senate Majority Leader Chuck Schumer screwing up Biden's agenda, bowing to Senate tradition, accepting the filibuster and letting it cripple the aspirations of her leftist cronies. They are seeing Schumer throw away the once-in-a-lifetime chance to profoundly change America and kindle a progressive revolution. So I think AOC just might emerge to challenge Schumer in the New York State Democratic Primary. He's up in 2022, and AOC would win if she ran. New York's politics is totally ethnic. She'd obviously carry Latinos, about a quarter of the vote, and likely, Blacks would come along, too. Jews, Schumer's base, have largely left the Democratic primary and become Republican. Those left in the Democratic primary are hardened leftists who have left their love of Israel—if they ever felt it—far behind. Indeed, pollster John McLaughlin probed the actual religious views of New York's Jews. He found that close to half self-identify as atheists or agnostics—not a likely constituency for Chuck.

Now take a step further into outer space with me.

Let's say she wins the primary, and of course, the general election. Her reputation as a giant killer will soar and her name will be on everyone's lips. Terrified that Trump would win in 2024, it's easy to see how Democrats might turn to AOC to save their party, especially if they lose Congress in 2022.

AOC might win primary after primary, inflaming the leftist grass roots with her charisma and radical agenda. And she's old enough . . . barely. Her birth date was October 13, 1989. She'll turn thirty-five, the minimum age specified in the Constitution to be president, three months before she would be sworn in if she won.

Could AOC actually win and ruin this beautiful country from a perch in the White House? Absolutely not. She'd likely lose more than forty states, and might lose all fifty. It would be George McGovern, Walter Mondale, or Mike Dukakis all over again.

But AOC's goal is not necessarily the presidency. The doctrine of the communists and radical left is, oddly, to destroy the moderate liberal party so there are no alternatives for centrists to embrace other than their radical faction. Just like it was in pre-Nazi Germany, where the center-left Catholic Party was discredited, leaving voters to face a choice between Nazism and Communism.

It may not happen. But it could.

PART III

The Message: Democrats Have Made America Unrecognizable

8

The Three Big Issues

THREE BIG ISSUES LOOK to dominate the political landscape as this is written: inflation, immigration, and crime.

Each of the three has the same unique feature: none was a problem under Donald Trump, and all emerged as serious issues on the day that Biden was inaugurated.

Inflation

Prices had been stable since the 1970s, when Biden came into office, rising by 2 percent or less each year. The experts at the Federal Reserve Board were more worried about deflation—the continuing drop in price and wages—rather than the opposite.

With the pandemic, resulting in shoppers staying home, and with workers not leaving their houses, both production and demand plummeted as the economy went into a yearlong hibernation.

When the Trump vaccine brought us out of hiding in the closing months of his administration, we all wondered what the recovery would look like.

We each chose a letter of the alphabet to symbolize what we thought would happen. Some worried that it would be a U-shaped recovery—a sharp downfall and then a long period of stagnation as the economy tried to recover. Trump predicted a V-shaped recovery—quickly down and quickly up.

It turned out that, once again, Trump was right. After the economy stopped shedding jobs, it came roaring back at a breathtaking pace.

Having lost an astounding twenty-two million jobs at the start of the pandemic, Trump's economy rebounded big time, adding back thirteen million jobs by the time he left office—a stunning pace of almost two million jobs a month!

Then things slowed down as fears of a possible Biden tax increase seized control of the markets. When Trump left office—nine months after the pandemic wave had engulfed us—we had already regained 59 percent of the lost jobs. But after seven months of Biden, we were still only up to 75 percent. Unemployment lingered. A U replaced a V in the calligraphy of our recovery.

Biden's Democrats thought they had the answer: the same one they always suggest—more government spending. They passed a $1.9 trillion stimulus package, and are trying to pass additional trillions.

By their logic, that level of spending should have sent the economy growing as if it were on steroids. But a new enemy had emerged, spawned from the residue of the Democrats' big spending—inflation.

Some of it was caused by Democratic policies. By killing the Keystone Pipeline, proclaiming an end to fossil fuels, stopping oil drilling offshore and in Alaska, and banning new fracking contracts on federal lands, their programs sent the price of gasoline and all energy soaring, from an average of $2.20 per gallon in November 2020, to $3.28 in May 2021, and is predicted to break four dollars by the end of the year.

Fear of Biden tax increases and tougher regulation reined in production. Who, for example, would be crazy enough to invest in new plant and equipment when Biden was proposing to double the capital gains tax?

Anxious to appease a public concerned about the slow pace of recovery, Biden and his Congress lavished voters with new goodies. They increased unemployment benefits by $300 more per week, gave every person a $1,400 stimulus check, increased food stamp aid, and paid out more in Obamacare subsidies. Economists calculated that if people stayed home and did not work, a family of four could make a pretax income of $100,000 a year just living off federal benefits. So why work?

Millions did the sensible thing and decided to stay home. Nine million jobs were unfilled by the end of summer 2021. It didn't pay to go to work. You made more by not working.

Supply bottlenecks began to choke off the recovery. Businesses couldn't find workers and had to pay much more to attract the few who were still willing to work. Oil was too expensive. The fear of new taxation loomed. Chips were in short supply. Parts weren't available. Foreign suppliers, whom we relied on during the pandemic, closed down due to COVID. The domestic firms that replaced them charged higher prices. Production slumped.

But meanwhile, consumer demand was on fire. The stimulus payments, the unemployment aid, and the money from other social programs seemed to burn a hole in our pockets as we raced to buy stuff to make up for the fallow days of the pandemic.

Too much demand and not enough supply. The predictable result: more inflation. After years of creeping upward at 2 percent or less each year, prices jumped up at an annual rate of 10 percent. We felt the inflation everywhere, at every store, every restaurant, every service, every block, every gas station. And the cause was, and is, obvious to us all: Biden's demented policies.

Immigration

When Biden was elected, it was fiesta day at the Mexican border. Barriers came down, and those who were arrested for crossing illegally were released, flown at government expense (often in secret) to new homes deep in the heartland of our country, often despite local objection. Border checks for COVID stopped, even as we Americans all had to continue to wear masks. Deportations stopped, even for those who had committed violent felonies while they were here illegally. Murderers and rapists were invited to stay. The Trump border wall stood incomplete, with plenty of room to slip through. Record amounts of fentanyl and other drugs poured over the border. Human trafficking resumed.

In June 2021, a record number of more than two hundred thousand illegal immigrants were caught sneaking in each month—and then were released or "resettled" into communities that did not want them. Six hundred unaccompanied children flocked over the border every day.

The borders were open! As the word spread through Mexican and Central-American communities, a record number bought illegal passage from coyotes.

Trump was gone!

But the issues that the mass illegal immigration has brought to our shores remain and fester. Tens of thousands arrived, unvaccinated, carrying the COVID virus with them. Demands for social services and overcrowding in local schools became acute.

Democrats privately celebrated, counting each new arrival as an extra vote. But America wasn't celebrating. Scenes of migrant children kept in cages, of a constant flow of migrants paddling across the Rio Grande in makeshift boats, rekindled the sense of anger and disgust that they thought Trump and his border wall had stopped. But now they were back!

Crime

And with it came rising crime. As the Democratic Left demanded cuts in police funding and new restrictions on what a cop could do, potential police recruits turned away, unwilling to risk public humiliation from the people they were trying to protect.

Crime was back on the front pages!

Nationally, we have experienced a 30 percent jump in murders—a record. And in the nine cities where the Left has cut the police budget, murders are up 68 percent.

And even now, new restrictions on police loom ahead. The Left wants to hold cops individually civilly liable for monetary damages if they infringe on anyone's constitutional rights. With these cases often tried before juries heavily weighted toward

minorities, what officer would not think twice about losing his pension, job, and home before making an arrest? Only those who did not lift a finger when the public was threatened assumed no risk.

None of these three plagues bothered us much under Trump. But they are now all here, under Biden—graphic and living proof of how misguided his policies and programs really are.

How to Frame Our Message

Despite their obvious severity, making our big three issues work for us in 2022 and 2024 will be a tricky business.

It's not easy to find an issue to bring down a president, much less to have three of them.

It's not enough to find issues on which you and your opponent disagree, even if they concern a vital area of great importance to the voters.

For an issue to work, it has to pass a three-part test:

- **Fault.** You have to prove that the problem is the other side's fault.
- **We'll do better.** You need to establish that you and your approach will do better at solving it.
- **Your opponent can't change his spots.** You've got to choose an issue on which your opponent will stick to his guns and not fudge or change his views when it is apparent that your attacks are scoring and gaining ground. Remember that an incumbent has many ways to duck your punches.

Consider how Obama slipped and slid out of issues that might otherwise have destroyed his popularity. Eight years of economic stagnation and virtually no economic growth could

have fatally wounded President Obama. But the economy, while it was of concern to all voters, never made it through the three-part test.

We never convinced the voters that the sluggish economy was Obama's fault. Coming off the crash of 2007 and 2008, he was able to blame Bush throughout his administration, so our punches never landed squarely. (At the time, Republicans were joking that Obama was going to rename California's San Andreas Fault, Bush's Fault.)

We also failed to establish that the Republicans would be able to do a better job. Bush's economic record was never that good, and his credibility on the issue was undermined by the economic collapse caused by the subprime scandal at the end of his second term.

Finally, we could not satisfy the third prong of the test: even when our attacks began to hit home, Obama was able to shift his ground, trim his positions, and move to the center.

But in 2024, we will be able to pass the three-part test with flying colors—on inflation, immigration, and crime. We can pin the blame on the Democrats and show that we did better when Trump was president, and the Biden record is so clear that he can't possibly wriggle out of blame.

Fault. It's obvious that the problems of inflation, immigration, and crime are all Biden's fault. They simply weren't problems before he took office.

For forty years, there had been little or no inflation. Then suddenly, prices for gas and almost everything else began to take a sharp rise. Sixty percent of voters, according to a Morning Consult poll, blame Biden for inflation, specifically citing his big spending proposals.[1]

And in a national poll by McLaughlin, 61 percent of voters agreed that the rapid growth of unemployment and other social benefits is also to blame for inflation. Even Democrats agreed by 47–30.

Crime, too, is obviously spreading on Biden's watch. Crime rates were minuscule during the first three years of the Trump administration, until the angry (and justified) outrage at the George Floyd murder—and the Democratic response to it— emasculated the police, sending murder rates up. Biden's push to cut police budgets and transfer spending from cops to social workers, his support for eliminating cash bail and ending mandatory sentences, all were misguided policies (from which Biden is now trying to run) that laid the basis for the meteoric rise in crime under Biden.

The case is even clearer that illegal immigration is Biden's fault. Before he dismantled Trump's immigration policies and stopped construction on his wall, illegal immigration had slowed to a trickle. Now, under Biden, it has become a torrent in less than one year.

The second prong? Proving that Trump would do better? That one is easy. We know that Trump *would* do better, because when he was president, he *did* do better. Coming off four years of no inflation, little illegal immigration, and for the first three years of his term, little rise in crime, who can disagree that Trump succeeded—and will again—where Biden failed?

Biden can't change his position. The Democrats are stuck with their record of inflation, illegal immigration, and rising crime, and no amount of maneuvering or clever talking points can get them out of it.

This particular leopard cannot change his spots. Biden would lose his progressive Democratic base if he tried. He is so firmly on record as demanding higher government spending and larger social benefits that he cannot reverse field. Nor will his leftist political base tolerate it if he backs away from his spending programs or their pet issues of climate change, Medicare expansion, and health insurance.

By the same token, the Left sees illegal immigration not as a problem, but as an opportunity. There would be hell to pay if Biden suddenly were to start enforcing the Southern border.

Neither would the Left look kindly on any Biden backsliding on his anti-police policies. His political base, particularly in the minority communities, would rebel quickly were he even to attempt it.

No, Joe Biden, Kamala Harris, and the entire Democratic Party are stuck with the trio of issues: inflation, immigration, and crime.

9

The Unrecognizable America

BY ANY MEASUREMENT, THE Democratic victory of 2020 was as narrow as it gets. The aftermath of the election—and the outrageous way paper ballots were handled in Georgia—left the Senate split evenly, 50/50, giving the Democrats control only through the rarely used power of the vice president to break a tie.

In the House, the Democrats lost ten seats and now hold power by only a nine-seat margin.

And of course, the victory of Joe Biden has been suspect from the beginning—and will probably become even more so when election audits are completed in Arizona, Georgia, and Wisconsin.

On the strength—or weakness—of these thin mandates, one would assume that the Democrats would have governed with an attitude of circumspection, and even modesty, given the controversial and narrow margin of their governing coalition.

But the Democrats did not settle for marginal changes, even as questions about the validity of their victory have swirled around the nation. Instead, they used their razor-thin Electoral College victory—which was won, in turn, by hotly disputed and extremely narrow wins in a handful of swing states—to propose the most radical and far-reaching agenda ever ventured by a major party in American history.

The radical, Marxist, and revolutionary forces that propped up a senile and dysfunctional Joe Biden demanded the enactment of legislation and executive action that would have so fundamentally altered our nation as to render it unrecognizable were they to have been enacted.

With party-line votes that made a mockery of the deliberative legislative process, the Democrats lock-stepped their narrow majorities on vote after vote to pass their radical agenda.

The myth of the moderate Democrat—or indeed, of the Democratic legislator who thinks for himself or herself—has been exposed in the process. There are not 225 Democratic members of the House, or 50 in the Senate. There are merely that many voting machines programmed to pass anything the leadership can conjure.

Only the solitary, courageous, and principled opposition of two Senators—Joe Manchin of West Virginia, and Kyrsten Sinema of Arizona—has stood in the way of the total destruction of America's finances, economy, electoral system, health care programs, racial justice and equality, voluntary unionization, educational systems, and the energy grid.

Their refusal to allow the barest fifty-vote margin to pass revolutionary legislation has proven to be an act of divine grace, sparing America from ruin.

Will these tender and slender reeds be able to withstand the tempest of the Democratic Left? That chapter of history is being written right now.

How odd it is that the filibuster, the very institution that has historically stood in the way of progress, should now be our salvation?

But however it turns out, we must vow, at the next election, to rescue our democracy from what its fate would be by delivering a convincing repudiation of the socialist governing program of the Democratic Party.

America is getting harder and harder to recognize. If it passes, the Democratic legislative program of 2021, rubber-stamped by the House, will transform our country into something we have never seen before.

Imagine what America would be like if the Left succeeds in enacting its dystopian legislation.

It's imperative to understand what the Left would do to us if it ever were to achieve a workable majority in both Houses.

So let's ponder for a moment, what the radical Left would—and almost has—inflicted on our country. Their proposals are so revolutionary as to make our nation unrecognizable to its citizens. Politically, the Left's agenda gives us fodder to retake our Congress in 2022. Simply enumerating the Democrats' incredible plans for the future will be an effective strategy for defeating them.

Look at how America is becoming unrecognizable under Biden and the Democrats.

Partisanship Becomes a Blood Sport

The lunatics have taken over the asylum. There's no other way to describe what happened when the Democrats acquired the majority in both Houses of Congress in 2020. Gone is the notion of consensus. And gone, too, is the idea of give-and-take.

Once, government shutdowns were rare—often just threatened as a negotiating tactic. Now, they've become the norm. The US Congress has not passed a budget in recent years, living year-to-year by ad hoc appropriations. The idea that you might do long-term planning is so "over" as to become quaint.

Any difference between the parties on legislation or spending is routinely resolved only by a government shutdown in which all federal workers are sent home, and most government agencies are closed. No passports. No national parks. No social services.

Then ensues a period of partisan rhetoric in which each side—through dueling daytime televised press conferences—blames the other for shutting the government down. Finally, after weeks, or even months, of government dysfunction, public opinion polls resolve the dispute by determining which party voters blame more for the shutdown, and make clear which has suffered more political harm.

And this charade is played out annually, unless one party controls both Congress and the White House.

Election Fraud Becomes Normalized

We would become a banana republic—much like governments in Central and South America and in Africa, where nobody knows who won the election—if the Senate were to follow the lead of the House and passes HR 1.

The electoral process would become unrecognizable. Even now, Election Day is no longer a big deal. Voting is stretched over weeks, and even months. And voters are increasingly able to cast ballots for days, or even weeks, after the polls are supposed to have closed.

The day after Election Day no longer matters much. We often don't know who won or lost an election until weeks, or even months, have passed, and until all absentee and mailed-in ballots have been counted as they trickle in—purposefully—at a snail's pace.

Disputed election results used to be rare. Even as he lost to Kennedy in 1960, by a tiny margin, amid valid accusations of voter fraud by the Daley machine in Chicago, Nixon did not contest the results since he was loath to send America into chaos.

No more. The dust has still not settled on the 2020 election, with its many documented charges of irregularities. The courts wouldn't intervene, and the public's faith in the electoral process was undermined.

There used to be few opportunities for voter fraud, since the rules were well-established. Only citizens could be registered, and only registered voters could cast ballots. With voting on Election Day *and* in person, the instances of fraud were rare.

Now, with more than half of the ballots submitted by mail, and virtually no checks to determine eligibility, or even the identity of voters, the ballot box is functionally open to anyone—even to people who don't exist or who have died, in whose names tens of thousands of votes are cast.

Once, you had to be a citizen to vote. Now, non-citizens are allowed to vote in local elections in many places in California, and potentially millions of non-citizens can illegally vote through loopholes in voter identification laws.

Where once, it was accepted practice to have to show photo identification to vote, now it is anathema, and seen by some as a gimmick to suppress minority turnout.

Before, those who were eligible to register to vote could do so with proper identification. Now, anyone who applies for welfare, Medicaid, food stamps, tuition assistance, or any form of government handout is automatically registered, regardless of whether they are eligible or not.

In the America we knew, anyone who was away on Election Day, and gave a reason, could cast an absentee ballot. Now, no reason is required, and absentee ballots have become a convenience rather than a necessity.

Once, violent felons were permanently barred from having a say in our laws and destiny. When you killed someone or committed another felony, you lost the privilege of voting to choose our leaders and laws. Now, that is called "felony disenfranchisement," and the Democrats seek to end it.

Most of these changes—revolutions, really—stem from the pandemic that gripped America in 2020, and whose damage lingers today. Democrats used the coronavirus to change almost everything in our beautiful country.

They were guided by the words and perverted wisdom of Rahm Emanuel, one of President Clinton's key aides, who became mayor of Chicago. He set down, for all time, the basic premise of the Democratic Party's plan to achieve power and radical change in America: "Never let a good crisis go to waste." Emanuel elaborated: "What I mean by that, is it's an opportunity to do things you think you could not do before."[1]

Even though, thankfully, the worst aspects of the radical left agenda proposed by Biden and passed by the Democratic automatons, who are the majority in the House of Representatives, appear to have been blunted in the Senate by the filibuster, their wild and radical proposals are still on the table and in their agenda.

Impeachment Becomes Routine

From the inception of our nation, the remedy of impeaching and removing an elected president from office has been an unthinkable idea. Only after the Civil War did enraged pro-Union Republicans take the extreme step of impeaching President Andrew Johnson for supporting the racist agenda of the fallen South. And even then, he was acquitted and served out his term.

But that reluctance to use the "nuclear option" of impeachment changed in 1974, when a US president was forced to resign under threat of removal.

In 1999, Republicans tried to impeach President Clinton on charges of lying under oath about having a sexual relationship with a young, but legally of age, woman. Fortunately, cooler heads prevailed, and the Senate refused to vote to convict him.

But impeachment became the norm. The Democratic House majority, with scarcely a Republican vote, tried it twice. Reversing an election through impeachment is becoming almost routine anytime the House—which has the power to initiate impeachment—is controlled by the opposite party.

The first impeachment attempt, in 2019, sought to oust President Trump for threatening the president of Ukraine with a cutoff of American aid unless he would cooperate with a partisan attempt to dig up dirt on Biden, who was moving toward the nomination as the Democratic candidate to oppose Trump in 2020.

The impeachment attempt ran into several obstacles:

- It turned out that it was Biden, not Trump, who had used his leverage as Obama's point man on dealings with Ukraine to get the Kiev regime to fire a prosecutor who was closing in on the corrupt relationship between Hunter Biden and the energy company Burisma. So the information that Trump was hoping the Ukrainian president would expose was, indeed, true.
- Trump did not actually threaten Ukraine with a cutoff of aid, but made a procedurally appropriate request that the government there turn over to US authorities any evidence that the former vice president's son—or that Biden himself—was involved in corrupt dealings with Burisma. The two countries—the United States and Ukraine—had a treaty pledging to share information about corruption, so the request was not out of bounds.
- After Trump's phone call—and after the president of Ukraine took no action to grant his request—US aid continued to flow, with no evidence of any retaliation.

Because Trump had done nothing wrong, the Senate acquitted him along party lines, with only one Republican—Senator Mitt Romney of Utah—voting to convict. Thus ended months of distraction, name-calling, and embittering partisanship.

The second Democratic attempt to oust Trump was even weirder in that it came after he had already left office, following the 2020 election, and after a mob had stormed the US Capitol on January 6, 2021, to protest against alleged fraud in the vote count.

The riot stemmed from the accumulated frustration and out-rage of millions of Americans at the utter failure of state leg-islatures, Congress, and the state and federal courts to even hear objections to the vote counting, and the lack of signature verification that made the 2020 election suspect. A national survey conducted in February 2021, found that 67 percent of Republicans believed that the election was "invalid," while only 23 percent disagreed.[2]

In a democracy, when two-thirds of the adherents of the los-ing party in a presidential election go so far as to say that they consider it to have been "invalid," the Capitol Hill mob could be forgiven for finding the refusal of the courts to intervene to be outrageous—as it indeed was. The entire judicial branches of our state and federal governments abdicated their responsibility by refusing to study, probe, or evaluate the claims of fraud—either rejecting them without fact-finding, or dismissing them on their face.

The various state trial courts, and failing that, the US District Court should have accepted the case and appointed a special master, equipped with a sizable budget, staff, and subpoena power to investigate the charges. Instead, they hid behind a lack of standing by the plaintiffs to duck the issue and do nothing. Such gross neglect of their most fundamental duty ranks as the worst failure of the judiciary since the Dred Scott decision of 1857, which forbade any restriction on the spread of slavery. That verdict led to a civil war. That the current malfeasance led to only a somewhat violent demonstration is an example of restraint, not of insurrectionist intent.

The Capitol Hill riot of January 6th gave the Democrats the pretext they needed to proceed with impeachment. Even though Trump had peacefully left office—after dozens of news stories speculated that he might not—the Democratic desire for revenge was so inflamed as to demand that he be kicked out on the way out. Everyone who observed the charade agreed that a conviction was not in the realm of political possibility, and that, even if that were to be the verdict, it would have no practical impact, since he had already left office.

But impeach they did, with the predictable result of acquittal.

The supposed ground for impeachment was the accusation that Trump had incited the January 6 riot by egging on the mob and making incendiary statements to urge violence. Impeachment advocates likened the president's remarks to the imaginary situation conjured by Supreme Court Justice Oliver Wendell Holmes Jr., in a 1919 decision holding that it was not a violation of the First Amendment to punish someone advocating opposition to the draft in World War I. Holmes said that such speech, in that overwrought situation, was like "shouting 'Fire!' in a crowded theater,"[3] and was not constitutionally protected.

The problem was that Trump had not only refrained from egging on the crowd, but had specifically urged them to disperse and go home.

Americans realized that the Left had gone too far by attempting to criminalize a presidential statement.

Trump was acquitted when only fifty-seven senators voted to convict—eleven short of the required two-thirds.

To their everlasting shame, the following ten Republican representatives voted to impeach:

- Liz Cheney, Wyoming
- Anthony Gonzalez, Ohio
- Fred Upton, Michigan

- Tom Rice, South Carolina
- Peter Meijer, Michigan
- John Katko, New York
- Adam Kinzinger, Illinois
- Jamie Herrera Beutlier, Washington
- Dan Newhouse, Washington
- David Valadao, California

And these seven Republican Senators voted to convict:

- Mitt Romney, Utah
- Bill Cassidy, Louisiana
- Richard Burr, North Carolina
- Pat Toomey, Pennsylvania
- Ben Sasse, Nebraska
- Susan Collins, Maine
- Lisa Murkowski, Alaska

They all deserve to be defeated in 2022, or whenever their terms are up.

Toomey and Burr, cowards to the end, are retiring before we can kick them out, having milked Trump for his support in getting themselves re-elected, and then jettisoning him when he became inconvenient.

Romney has never gotten over his jealousy and envy that Donald Trump succeeded where he failed.

Bill Cassidy, who coasted to re-election in Louisiana in 2020, on the ticket led by Donald Trump, turned on the president after he secured his seat by pledging him fealty. Like Julius Caesar's Brutus, he knifed him in the end. For that, he was censured by the Louisiana Republican Party, which likely will be lying in wait for him in 2026, when he runs again.

Ben Sasse of Nebraska is just a Democrat who disguises himself in Republican red. He's not even a RINO. He's just a Democrat trying to steal votes by masquerading as a Republican in a totally red state.

Susan Collins, the seventh Republican who tried to kick Trump when he was down, is not worthy of reproach. She comes from Maine, one of the most liberal states in America—and one of the most dependent on government handouts. She makes no secret of her independence from Trump. She advertises it. That's how she can survive in Maine. She clings to her political life with the tenacity of an endangered species. All the other New England Republican senators have vanished. Senator Judd Gregg (NH) is gone. And so are Jim Jeffords (VT), Ed Brooke (MA), and Olympia Snowe (ME). Only Collins remains.

Whenever Collins stands accused of apostasy, remember to cut her a break. She comes from a solidly blue state and stays in office by walking on eggshells to re-election in order to keep the Senate Republican. God bless her.

Liz Cheney and Lisa Murkowski, however, are another matter.

Liz Cheney: The Bush Empire Strikes Back

For all of its folksy, WASPish, casual modesty, the Bush family is the most presumptuous and pretentious crowd in our recent history. Spawned by Senator Prescott Bush of Connecticut in the 1950s, they assume the presidency is their right, and the White House part of their inherited property.

Not only do they feel themselves entitled to be the first father-son team in the presidency since the Adams family, but they hold it against Trump that he blocked brother Jeb in his bid to make it a trifecta in 2016.

They have never forgiven Trump for belittling "low-energy Jeb," and for ridiculing his credentials.

All the king's horses and all the king's men rallied to Jeb's side when he ran. The formidable Bush money machine was there all the way. At a fundraiser at the Bush family compound in Kennebunkport, Maine, Jeb announced that he had already raised $103 million from super PACs, as well as $700,000 a day for his campaign coffers during the first two weeks of his candidacy.[4]

But Jeb stalled out, and deprived of their rightful sinecure, the Bush family was not amused. Neither Bush 41 nor Bush 43 backed Trump, even after he won the Republican nomination, and the younger former president announced that he had written in a candidate other than Trump in the general election.

But it fell to Liz Cheney, the former vice president's daughter, to exact revenge. Coming from the single most Republican state in the nation, Wyoming, she couldn't afford to knock the top of the ticket in the 2020 race. So she posed as a Republican, dutifully backing the president until her own re-election was ensured, and then turned on Trump and demanded his removal. She faced disciplining by her House colleagues, who removed her from leadership to punish her disloyalty.

We hope she gets what is coming to her in 2022.

Lisa Murkowski: Opportunist, Traitor, Turkey

The most prominent Republican defector during the second Trump impeachment was Alaska's Senator Lisa Murkowski.

She got her Senate seat from Daddy. Frank Murkowski ran for governor of Alaska while serving as its US senator in 2002. After his election, he resigned his Senate seat so he could appoint daughter Lisa in his place. Voters had no say in this swap. Alaskans were outraged and expressed themselves by voting, in a referendum, to strip future governors of the right to directly appoint replacement Senators.

In 2010, the Republicans of Alaska then rejected Lisa when she sought re-election, nominating instead, a Tea Party candidate, Joe Miller, who is also a former federal magistrate judge. Miller, who had Sarah Palin's support, beat Murkowski in the primary, but ambitious Lisa was not to be denied the Senate seat that she had inherited.

Murkowski decided to mount a write-in campaign against Miller—who was the Republican nominee—and Scott McAdams, the Democrat. She was funded massively by the state teachers and other public employee unions, and the entire establishment of the Alaska GOP—many of whom owed their positions to Lisa's Daddy.

Murkowski eventually won, but not before she was engulfed in a controversy over the hand-counting of paper ballots. Eventually, Murkowski was declared the winner by fewer than two thousand votes, amid charges by the Miller campaign that many of the write-in votes given to her were illegible or misspelled.

Miller cited Alaska law, which said that write-in ballots "may not be counted unless marked in compliance with the election rules." They quoted the Alaska statute: "The rules set out in this section are mandatory and there are no exceptions to them."[5]

But the courts, many of whose judges had been appointed or nominated by Governor Murkowski, ruled otherwise and certified Lisa as the winner.

So even as she entered the controversy surrounding Trump's supposed defeat by Joe Biden, Lisa had a history of riding dubious paper-ballot voting into power.

Now she runs for re-election in 2022, facing Donald Trump's explicit opposition. Kelly Tshibaka, the current Alaskan Commissioner of Administration under GOP Governor Mike Dunleavy, has announced that she will oppose Murkowski, with the blessing and support of President Trump. Happy hunting!

How to Use the Impeachment Issue to Win

Both parties have misused the ultimate sanction of impeachment. The two vain attempts to oust Donald Trump were, just as destructive as the Republican effort to replace Bill Clinton over the Monica Lewinsky scandal.

Each futile attempt distracted our attention from a crucial national crisis. In our book *Off With Their Heads!,* Eileen and I document how the GOP impeachment of 1999 distracted and weakened President Clinton at the crucial moment when we had Osama bin Laden in our sights. Rather than pull the trigger and kill him before he slaughtered over three thousand of us, Clinton dithered and let the chance pass. Under intense political fire over Monica, Clinton was worried that collateral civilian casualties might further undermine his presidency. Since bin Laden was then unknown to the American public, he saw no reason to risk popular vilification. He also worried that a cynical public would dismiss an attack on bin Laden as merely an attempt to "wag the dog" to distract Americans from his own impeachment.

As much as he deserves blame, so, too, do those who used a sex scandal to divert our attention from our real threats and problems.

Similarly, with our country awash in partisan and racial tension, and threatened by the COVID pandemic, the Democrats exaggerated the actions of an uncontrolled mob to try to convince America that it had been on the verge of an insurrection, encouraged and fomented by the president. Trump neither approved, nor even countenanced, the riot of January 6. Using it as a pretext for impeachment only served to embitter half the country and to make a mockery of Biden's futile preaching of unity in his subsequent inaugural address. It cast a pall over his swearing-in, and blocked any serious investigation of Democratic tactics in the election itself, to the detriment of the entire country.

Those who waste our time and try to turn molehills into mountains, distracting us from public purpose, deserve to pay a political price.

The Republican Party paid just such a price in the elections of 1998, when the partisan venom of the GOP backfired and caused the party of the incumbent president to lose seats in the by-election for the first time in American history.

It remains to be seen if voters will inflict similar punishment on the Democratic and RINO sponsors of Trump's impeachment.

Refusing to Negotiate on Legislation

Negotiation lies at the core of our system of checks and balances. Our entire political system is designed to foster it, and to require it. But now, negotiation and compromise are anathema in the new, unrecognizable America the Democrats are creating.

Our Founding Fathers—in the eighteenth century—had a very different view of democracy from that of their contemporary revolutionary colleagues in France. There, Enlightenment philosophers felt that it was the duty of government to heed what they called the "general will." So they developed a political system in which there were no checks and balances, but the popular will ruled the day. Every day.

By contrast, our Founders were skeptical of the "general will," and worried that it could be too easily inflamed by passion and prejudice. So they developed a constitutional system designed to enable—but also to thwart—the popular will by making it wait until after passions had cooled to be enacted.

This suspicion of the general will led to their decision to stagger the terms of presidents, senators, and congressman so that one election could not completely change the government. While congressmen—the core of representative democracy— were elected every two years, senators were elected every six, and presidents every four.

Our democracy and constitution have lasted since 1788, while France's has been through five republics and several dictatorships and monarchies during that period. The decision of our Founders would appear to have been the right one.

By denying our public officials the possibility of immediately translating an election victory into new law without passing it through checks and balances, the Constitution demands negotiation.

But in our era of polarized politics and deep suspicion between the parties, negotiation has become synonymous with selling out. Both parties often try to sweep out the old order and install a new one. And from time to time, such a transformative election does indeed happen, as it did in 2008 (for the Democrats), 2010 (for the Republicans), and in 2020 (for the Democrats).

The election of 2008 was a clear Democratic mandate, sweeping in Barack Obama as president and flipping Congress. Voters demanded an end to the war in Iraq, and they got it.

In 2010, it was the Republicans' turn for what was called a "realignment election," with a net gain of six Senate and sixty-three House seats. They passed fundamental reforms on how the chamber functioned, and less successfully, tried to rein in Obamacare.

In 2020, of course, there was no mandate for anything. Biden was narrowly elected—if that—and the Democrats lost a net of ten seats in the House, while still keeping a narrow majority. Democrats did retake the Senate, but only the vote of VP Kamala Harris could break the 50/50 tie and bring them to power.

But despite the narrow margin of their victories, the Democrats have chosen to try to enact the most radical agenda of all time. Normally, in our politics, when a party wins only narrowly, it's mission is clear: move to the center to get more votes. But the Democrats did the opposite, veering sharply to the left even more than they had during the election.

To be fair, Democratic Party leaders didn't have much choice but to veer sharply to the left. Their own voters would have found anything less than the radical Biden program unacceptable. The Party leadership had to remember that out-and-out Socialist Bernie Sanders (he wasn't even a Democrat) almost won their presidential nomination.

For their part, the Republicans didn't have much leeway for compromise either. In 2016, Donald Trump had come out of nowhere to win the nomination over many opponents with long political resumes. Advocating "America First," Trump won with policies that defied the longstanding GOP commitment to free trade, and broke with the Eisenhower-Bush-Kissinger tradition of close consultation with our allies. He won by rolling over the traditional conservative favorite, Texas Senator Ted Cruz, and the establishment choice, Florida's Governor Jeb Bush.

So the Republicans and Democrats had moved to their Right and Left extremes respectively as 2020 dawned, and the grounds for compromise and bipartisanship almost evaporated.

The way our congressional districts are drawn catalyzed this polarization.

The leaders of each party are so eager to protect their congressmen that they have made sure that the new congressional districts that must be drawn every decade, after the census, did not lead to their defeat by the opposite party.

Instead, they have seen to it that the reapportionment filled all districts represented by Democratic members with Democrats, and all Republican districts with Republicans. The number of swing districts has declined dramatically. Congressmen are no longer as afraid of defeat in the general election as they are of losing their primaries.

Nate Silver, of *The New York Times*, writes that there were 103 swing House districts in 1992. Today, there are fewer than than 40.[6]

Congressional reapportionment is controversial in most states, made the more so because of judicial review that often tosses out gerrymandered districts. Neither party likes it when the court pre-empts it in drawing new district lines after each census. The politicians in each party have their own scores to settle and would rather draw the lines themselves than let the courts do it.

So the two parties cut deal after deal between them in the various state legislatures. The underlying idea was, "I'll scratch your back if you scratch mine." Nervous Republicans were happy to fill their districts with red voters, while Democrats packed blue supporters into theirs.

In 2021, the Supreme Court, under the leadership of Chief Justice John Roberts, has declined repeatedly to intervene to stop partisan gerrymandering, claiming that it is a political question and outside its purview.

So gerrymandering made general elections into non-events. But with so many voters from their own parties now in their districts, intra-party primaries became more serious.

Congressmen got stiff necks looking over their shoulders at their own voter base, more worried about primary challenges than about their opponents in the other party.

It was the unique genius of Donald Trump to use this polarization to whip Republican congressmen and senators into line behind him by leveraging his vast support among the grassroots. Faced with the possibility of primaries, they knuckled under and did what Trump wanted.

But Biden had no such grassroots support in his party. The primaries of 2020 showed that he was not popular among the party faithful (he lost all three early primaries). He only won by the support of the Black leadership in the primaries, and the organized Left in the general election. So he could not use the partisan polarization to his advantage like Trump could. Instead, he became hostage to the extreme Left rather than be their leader. It was they who elected him, and they owed Biden nothing. All the powerless Biden could do was to lamely and tamely follow the extreme Left and become their puppet. This imbecility led Biden and the Democrats into a radical left-wing cul de sac from which they cannot escape.

But neither party seeks compromise. The Democrats, because they can't—their base won't permit it. The Republicans, because they needn't—their partisan agenda is too popular.

While Black and radical elements took over the Democratic Party, Trump led the Republicans Party to major success as its policies moved America toward a roaring economy, energy independence, a narrowing of the rich/poor divide, well-enforced borders, and greater international security.

But the Left pushed the Democrats to adopt huge spending bills, a racially polarized agenda, a subordination of feminism to pro-gay legislation, open borders, and the radical Green Agenda.

In this environment, the Democrats moved sharply to the Left while Republicans gloried in the leadership of Donald Trump.

There is no longer any real basis for compromise on issues in today's politics. Neither side will allow it.

Now, Republicans can ride the Trump policies and record to a recovery in the elections of 2022 and 2024, while Democrats are stuck in a morass of their own making.

10

It's All About Race and Gender

L ET'S START WITH RACE—EVERYTHING now is about race. Even as race disappears from the American demographic—due to inter-racial marriage—our politics has become polarized around race and issues of privilege and discrimination.

After the civil rights movement of the '60s, race seemed to be on its way out as a dividing line in our society. Blessedly, integration was the order of the day, and with racial lines more blurred than ever. Some said, with justification, that we were entering a post-racial era.

Today, about nine million people live in bi-racial households, including large numbers of African Americans.

But despite the demographics, race is back, stronger than ever, as a dividing line in our politics and society. The idea of a colorblind America is farther from reality now than it has ever been.

Segregation has made an astonishing comeback. No longer is it the exclusive province of racist Southern Democrats and the Ku Klux Klan. Now, it is openly embraced and spread by the leftist academic, corporate, and political elite.

Recently, the graduation festivities at Columbia University were strictly segregated into separate ethnic and racial categories for African Americans, Latinos, gays, poor people, and Asian Americans. Each had their own ceremonies. (It is unclear whether those who fell into more than one category would get two degrees!)

In Wellesley, Massachusetts, the leftist school board seeks to bring back racial segregation—in effect, disregarding the Supreme Court's landmark 1954 decision in *Brown v. Board of Education*, outlawing it. The board divides students into "affinity groups" based on race, gender, and sexual preference, and does not let them cross-pollinate, much less integrate.

Legislation passed by a radical left-wing Congress and some Democratic states now specifically designates certain laws, rules, programs, and expenditures as only for Black people (or "people of color") as opposed to white Americans. Increasingly, everything is seen through the prism of race.

In 2021, Congress passed Biden's stimulus program, which contained a $5 billion program available only to "people of color" in rural areas. $4 billion was for the purchase of seeds, fertilizer, and farm equipment, or to pay back debts. And $1 billion was earmarked for scholarships . . . but again, only for people of color. Whites need not apply.

Antonio Vitello, the owner of Jake's Bar and Grill in Harriman, Tennessee, applied for aid from Biden's Restaurant Relief Fund after being forced to close during the COVID lockdown. But the program's administrators—under the Small Business Administration (SBA)—gave priority to "grants to businesses owned by women and racial minorities."[1] So they only accepted loan applications from businesses owned by "people of color" for the first twenty-one days.

Vitello himself is a white Italian American, but his wife, a half-owner of the business, is Hispanic. However, since she only owns half the business—not 50 percent—the restaurant did not qualify as owned by people of color. By the time the twenty-one days were up, and applications from whites could finally be accepted, the $29 billion allocated by Congress to the fund had run out, and the loan window was closed.

Because the Vitellos naively believed that, as Americans, they could not legally face discrimination based on skin color, they reached out to the Wisconsin Institute for Law & Liberty (WILL), which filed a suit on their behalf in the federal district court.

In a harbinger of things to come, the Vitellos won by a 2–1 vote, and now similar lawsuits are proliferating around the country.

Meanwhile, a legal group founded by ex-Trump aide Stephen Miller (one of the best) filed another lawsuit accusing the Biden administration of racial discrimination in the distribution of COVID-19 relief funds for restaurant owners.

Miller argued that "as these restaurant owners, operators and workers try to pick up the pieces and rebuild their businesses [after COVID], they are facing a new and insidious threat: Racial discrimination from the government." He wrote that the "decision from the Biden Administration to determine eligibility and priority for restaurant relief funds based upon race is profoundly illegal and morally outrageous."[2]

And the reverse racism continues. On June 15, 2021, Vice President Kamala Harris joined Biden's secretary of the treasury, Janet Yellen, in launching a $1.25 billion program of aid to small businesses under the Rapid Recovery Program.

Correction: not aid to small businesses, but only to *minority- and female-owned* small businesses.

Harris, defending the priority based on race, said: "Traditional banks do not always understand the visions of businesses owned by women, people of color, or serve low-income areas, but community lenders do."[3]

Back in the sixties and seventies, Black Muslims, led by Elijah Mohammed and Malcolm X, rejected integration and touted Black supremacy. But now, in our new unrecognizable America, this twisted, racist thinking lies at the core of both the current civil rights movement and much federal legislation. Shame on the Left!

Like the Vitellos did, we can expect thousands of white-owned businesses, left out in the cold by race-based programs, to file a deluge of lawsuits challenging the constitutionality of race-specific programs. Already, the courts have thrown out several of these programs because they are, obviously, in violation of the Equal Protection Clause of the Fourteenth Amendment.

In today's politics, it's CRT vs. MLK—Critical Race Theory advocating segregation, defying Dr. Martin Luther King Jr.'s insistence on integration.

The Racist: Critical Race Theory

Democratic race-based policies are especially destructive. Think for a minute about what they are doing to the underlying fabric of our society.

What are fourth-grade white children to think when Critical Race Theory, taught in schools with federal funding (and often required by state mandate), tells them that their Black mother is being exploited by their white father? Or that everything his or her family has owns came by exploiting people of color? Oedipal theory holds that boys want to marry their mothers and kill their fathers. How does that destructive psychological imperative intersect with Critical Race Theory ideology?

What would Critical Race Theory do to marital stability? What are the consequences for parents trying to lead stable and colorblind lives?

The Left has drawn a line in the sand to distinguish equity from equality. While we have come to see these terms as synonyms, leftist dogma holds that they are, instead, opposites.

Equality means the treatment of all people equally, regardless of race.

To the new, racist Left, that dream is a nightmare.

They prefer to emphasize *equity*, in which people of color are given preference over whites to compensate for past injustice and discrimination, presumably going back nine generations to their great-great-great-great-great-great-great-grandfather's enslavement.

Paula Dressel of the leftist Race Matters Institute wrote, "The route to achieving equity will not be accomplished through treating everyone equally. It will be achieved by treating everyone justly according to their circumstances."[4]

In that dichotomy, the Biden administration casts its lot—and its money—decisively behind equity and rejects equality. While a number of states have banned Critical Race Theory from being taught in public schools, the radical Left is incentiv-izing it by federal grants.

Over the summer of 2021, the Biden administration's Department of Education funded a virtual Equity Summit Series, which aims to urge schools to "infuse equity into all of their work."[5]

Advocating Racial Equality to Win the Election

In the elections of 2022 and 2024, the Republican Party should run as the party of Martin Luther King, explicitly embracing his doctrine of equality, and rejecting the Black Lives Matter idea of equity. Our campaign should highlight the difference between the leftist ideology of the Black Lives Matter movement (BLM) and traditional civil rights values espoused by Dr. King (MLK).

A survey taken by McLaughlin & Associates in May 2021, found that, while Democrats embraced the idea of equity, Independents and Republicans rejected it in favor of equal-ity. McLaughlin found that, given a choice between Candidate A, who favors "equity to compensate for past injustices," and Candidate B, who insists that the law not favor one race, and that it must be colorblind, voters choose Candidate B by 66–29. (Democrats break about even, 49–44, in favor of race-based preferences.)

Politically, that the Democratic base is so at variance with the opinion of the rest of the country, makes equity versus equality a magnificent issue for the Republicans to use in 2022 and 2024. In any political campaign, it is particularly beneficial to find an issue where one's opponent's voters go one way, and the rest of the country goes the other.

Then your opponent has to stand firm on his unpopular views rather than trim or change them to accommodate public opinion. Were he to try to do so, he would alienate his own base. So he is stuck with his position and must defend it throughout the campaign, losing more and more voters along the way. His feet are stuck in cement.

The McLaughlin survey also found that the central tenet of Critical Race Theory—that the United States is a racist nation—is soundly rejected by American voters. By 54–36, they say it's not true, and by a like margin, object to teaching Critical Race Theory in schools.

And most American voters are dead set against granting reparations for slavery—a key demand of the Left. By 61–27, they agree with the statement that "the three hundred thousand white Union soldiers who died in the Civil War have been reparation enough, and that nothing is accomplished by paying for damage done eight generations ago." But Democrats have a blind spot on the issue, and back reparations by 50–34, even as all other Americans reject the idea.

Gender Becomes a Matter of Opinion

Now let's look at gender. Of all the nutty policies the Left is trying to foist on us, the most absurd is its attempt to change our gender and sexuality.

Even as the radical Left tries to elevate racial issues to make them politically pivotal, it seeks to gloss over gender differences in deference to the LGBTQ community (lesbian, gay, bi, transgender, and *queer*—their word, not mine).

They go to absurd lengths to eliminate gender from the national language, even as they highlight race. Their linguistic acrobatics led Biden's Health and Human Services secretary, Xavier Becerra, to tell the Senate Finance Committee that the administration used the word "birthing person" instead of "mother" in the Biden administration's $6 trillion budget.

Senator James Lankford (R-OK) grilled the secretary, saying that he "noticed you changed a term in your budget, where you shifted in places from using the term 'mother' to 'birthing people' rather than 'mother.'" He asked, "Can you help me get a good definition of 'birthing people'?"

Caught in a linguistic trap of his own making, Becerra answered, "I'll check on the language there, but I think if we're talking about those who give birth, I think we're talking about—I don't know how else to explain it to you."

The Biden administration's proposed Fiscal Year 2022 budget uses the term "birthing people," saying that the proposal includes funding for maternal health to "help end this high rate of maternal mortality and race-based disparities in outcomes among birthing people."

In its news coverage of the hearing, *The Washington Times* felt constrained to explain that the term "birthing person" has been "increasingly employed on the Left to avoid offending, for example, transgender people who give birth but do not identify as women, prompting eye-rolling on the Right."[6]

To jump through hoops to satisfy the radical demands of its gay and trans supporters, the Left has had to stake out positions that not only directly contradict the obvious reality into which we are all born, but also seek to nullify the traditional feminist agenda—even as they break from the historic civil rights movement goal of integration.

Their move away from support for the feminist agenda gives Republicans and conservatives great ammunition for the coming campaigns.

This new craziness finds its ultimate expression in the Left's support for transgender athletes competing against girls in school sports.

Standing the language on its head, the Biden administration takes the position that the statutory prohibition in Title IX of the civil rights law against "discrimination on grounds of sex or gender," bans efforts to separate transgender girls from biological girls in school sports.

That girls cannot compete with boys, or boys-turned-girls (transgender), is the core reason that female sports are separated from their male counterparts in scholastic and college competition in the first place.

In Connecticut, for example, boys who announced that they were really girls (often without either surgery or hormone therapy) were allowed to compete in track and field against real girls. The trans athletes won all the championships at stake, even defeating girls who had won medals competing against other girls before the transgender athletes were allowed into the races.

Alanna Smith, a sixteen-year-old African-American girl who is the daughter of Hall of Fame baseball pitcher Lee Smith, won the 100-meter Connecticut state championship three times in a row—in the sixth, seventh, and eighth grades—and in high school, she set records with her speed.

But then she hit a wall. As a freshman in high school, everything changed. Suddenly, she had to compete against boys. At the all-important State Open, she knew she could win against the girls, but now she had to race against a new opponent— Terry Miller, a middle-of-the pack runner in high school who hadn't even qualified for the nationals. But Terry was a boy. He and his friend, who is now called Andrea Yearwood, crossed over from boys sports to girls track and field. Among the boys, they were also-rans. But among the girls, they were champs.

How were they able to make the switch? Surgery? Hormones? Nope. In Connecticut, they just had to decide that they really were girls, after all. Just cross the street.

The result? Terry and Andrea placed first and second in the 100-meter race at the Connecticut State Open Finals.

Asking girls to compete with boys in track would be like adding a high-school athlete to an elementary-school competition.

So despite training heart-and-soul through long, grueling practices, Alanna just couldn't win. "Inside," she said, "I felt I had no chance of winning despite the hours of training and knowing my personal bests in each event. I was defeated before stepping onto the track. I knew it wasn't fair to me or to any of the other girls competing at the State Open. I knew I had biologically advantaged competition running against me."[7]

She continued: "It's hard to ignore the physical differences between us when we are lined up in the starting blocks, and so, mentally we know the outcome before the race even starts. We train so hard to compete, and yet some of the runners we are up against are not equal in physiology or experience. That biological unfairness doesn't go away because of what someone believes about gender identity."[8]

It wasn't just Alanna's problem. In the two and a half years that transgender boys have been allowed to compete against girls in Connecticut high-school sports, they won all fifteen Connecticut track and field championships. Middle-of-the-pack transgender boys beat the very best females. In fact, every year, there are numerous high-school transgender boys who can beat the times of adult, fully grown world champion Olympic female athletes.

At stake for Alanna is more than a medal and some glory.

College athletic scholarships often depend on a girl's performance at meets like this one.

Alanna and three of her friends sued then Connecticut Interscholastic Athletic Conference to keep girls sports for girls. The American Civil Liberties Union, which apparently doesn't think girls have rights, opposed the suit.

For decades, girls sports have gotten second-class treatment. They were something of a joke. Only 15 percent of high-school athletes were women. Men's sports were taken seriously, but girls were not. And guess what? The men got almost all the scholarships to colleges and universities.

Then, to stop this discrimination, in 1972, Congress passed the federal civil rights law, Title IX, as part of the Education Amendments Act, providing:

> No person in the United States shall, on the basis of sex, be excluded from participation in, be denied the benefits of, or be subjected to discrimination under any education program or activity receiving Federal financial assistance.

That opened the floodgates to girls sports. Today, there are 3.2 million girls competing in high-school athletics. And now, they win over 40 percent of athletic scholarships.

But then boys began to change their gender identity to become girls. The Connecticut rules say that a boy or girl can compete in the event that is appropriate for their "gender identity." Biology has nothing to do with it. If a boy says he's a girl, he's a girl. And suddenly, his chances of winning a scholarship skyrocket.

Of course, it's about a whole lot more than money. Many girls, like many kids, derive a lot of their self-esteem by winning at sports. But if the game is rigged, and they can't win, what does that do to them psychologically?

A high-school girl's self-esteem is often based on how she performs in comparison to her friends, academically and in sports. The experience of competing and winning is a key part of building her self-confidence. If she had to compete against bigger, stronger, and faster boys—and lose every time she played—it would be devastating.

The debate over transgender sports has often been confused with questions of gay rights and homosexuality. But this fight is different. It's not about kids changing their gender identity. That's legally their right. But now, by throwing transgender boys into athletic competition with girls, we are discriminating against girls. The rights of transgender boys are being elevated above those of the girls. Ideology is taking the place of biology. There are well-established differences between boys and girls in physical capacity. To require them to compete together leads to a foregone conclusion: the boys will win.

Biden and the radical Left will have it no other way. Tossing feminism out the window, they are catering to the LGBTQ pressure group. They are now pushing the so-called Equality Act in Congress. What a fraud! It doesn't promote equality. It gives transgender boys and men the advantage over girls and women. These boys-turned-girls are, in the words of George Orwell, "more equal than others."[9]

But the radical Left's bias against biological girls and women doesn't end with sports. Leftists insist on promoting radical gender-change surgery, even in children as young as ten, eleven, or twelve. The Biden administration even supports paying for such surgery with Medicaid funds.

In the trans world, the big danger is that a child's "biological" gender will not comport with his or her "gender identity." In other words, boys may want to be girls, and vice versa. Rather than seeing these adolescent fads for what they are, the trans community is pushing to perform gender-change surgery on pre-pubescent children to bring their biological sex into line with their identities.

These risky operations result in lifetime sterility about a quarter of the time.

The trans community says that it is necessary to perform the operations before puberty to avoid the risk of suicide. But data show that the leading cause of suicide among transgender kids is actually regret over having had gender-change surgery.

The Left maintains that, as CNN political reporter Devan Cole ridiculously said, "It's not possible to know a person's gender identity at birth, and there is no consensus criterion for assigning sex at birth."[10]

When my niece was eight years old, she asked her mother, "How do you tell if a baby is a boy or a girl?" Her mother patiently replied, "Think about it a bit." Then enlightenment dawned, and my niece's face lit up because she had the answer: "An extra Y chromosome."

Nobody disputes the right of any adult to change their gender or do what they wish with their own body, but we should, and must, draw the line at inflicting what amounts to castration on boys, and potentially, sterility on girls, particularly when they are too young to give informed consent.

The operations cost about $100,000 and are very, very hard to reverse, if they can be reversed at all.

To turn a girl into a boy, they lengthen her clitoris, extend her urethra, and make a scrotum.

Turning a boy into a girl involves breast augmentation and vaginoplasty, surgically creating a vulva and vaginal canal.

Infections, difficulty in wound healing, and possible sterilization are the worries for adult patients. But in children at such a young age, one of the major concerns is whether they can give informed consent. This is like a tattoo that never wears off.

The American College of Pediatricians says, "given the cognitive and experiential immaturity of the child and adolescent, we find the procedure to be highly problematic and unethical."

It goes on to point out that "Neuroscience clearly documents that the adolescent brain is cognitively immature and lacks the adult capacity needed for risk assessment."[11]

So how do kids get to this point?

Social pressure and peer group dynamics have a lot to do with it. One recent study says that kids often decide they are transgender after binging on social media sites like Tumblr, Reddit, and YouTube. They even have "coming out" parties to celebrate. It's cool. Like dying your hair orange or piercing every part of your body. It gets attention and acceptance from others in the LGBTQ community. Most of these kids, the study found, have mothers who encourage trans behavior. Some moms who wanted a girl and got a boy act out by cross-dressing their sons as girls.

Psychologists say that most trans pre-teenagers are very close to their mothers. They tend to have only peripheral relationships with their fathers.

The Left likes to pretend that biology is the cause of trans identification. They grieve over boys trapped in girls' bodies, and vice versa. But in studies of genetically identical twins, environmental factors account for three-quarters of those who turn trans. Biology only causes a quarter.

Among those kids who are subjected to gender-altering surgery, the die is cast. They are stuck for life. The others? Ninety percent of those kids who want the operations but can't get them (either because of cost or parental objection) accept their biological gender by late adolescence, the bulk of them right after puberty.

Despite the risk of sterilization, there are more than forty clinics around the country pushing gender-altering surgery, often for kids.

And Biden, ever obedient to his radical-Left handlers, signed an executive order during his first week in office, overturning Trump's decision not to let federal funds be used for transgender surgery in the military.

Biden even had the Department of Justice file an appeal in federal court so he could crack down on doctors and hospitals that won't do these operations. In one of his Orwellian turns of phrase, he calls their refusal "sex discrimination."

Generally, insurance won't cover transgender surgery without a psychiatric diagnosis of gender dysphoria for adults. But Medicaid foots the bill for transgender surgery in the twenty-two states that cover it. Eleven states prohibit Medicaid coverage of gender-change surgery. The rest have no legislated policy.

Surgical gender change on pre-pubescent children, using our tax money to pay for it—such is the fate that awaits us if the Democrats get to pass their radical program.

Using The Gender Issue to Win the Election

In our era of massive turnout, it may be futile to expect the average voter to grasp the complexities of issues like economics. But even the least educated among us know about gender differences and intuitively rebels at the Left's effort to make gender a choice, not a biological fact. They know crazy when they see it.

But the fact is that the gains of the two great social movements of the post-World War II era are now being undone at the hands of the Democrats: racial equality and feminism.

We watch radicals call for a resumption of segregation and racism, now directed against white people. The fundamental doctrine of equality is now under assault.

Likewise, the central idea behind feminism is threatened by the Left: the notion of female empowerment.

No longer does the Left stand for women's rights. It has subordinated them to gay and trans rights. In school athletics and gender-change surgery, it has adopted the agenda of the LBGTQ movement, scrapping the accomplishments of the likes of Betty Friedan, Billie Jean King, Gloria Steinem, and Bella Abzug.

The Republican Party of 2022 and 2024 needs to plant its flag squarely on the grounds of racial equality and feminism abandoned by the Democrats. By supporting racial equality in the face of demands for racial discrimination and segregation to offset the effects of prior injustice, we can occupy the high ground on the issue.

And by standing for girls sports, female empowerment, and achievement, we can pre-empt the issues that have animated the gender gap that has propelled the Democrats since the early 1970s.

Democrats Abandon the Middle Ground

Our political playing field has moved so far to the left that the fifty-yard line is now in the end zone. One after another, the Democrats have abandoned the fundamental tenets of our national dialogue.

Now it's up to the Republicans to seize the ground the Democrats have abandoned.

As a result of the incredible leftward tendency of today's Democratic Party, words that once had lost their meaning and become clichés in our political dialogue, have become hot buttons that sharply divide the parties from each other.

Democrats have abandoned the goal of racial equality in favor of the demented notion of racial equity—a doctrine based on the injustices of the past three hundred years rather than anything that is happening now.

To say that government should be colorblind, and schools racially integrated, has become a radical, inflammatory position, inviting at least a sharp debate, and perhaps, a riot.

Similarly, the idea of feminism, so deeply embedded in our culture, is now subordinate to the goal of elevating transgender people above women. The rights of gays and trans people have become more important than those of women or girls. Two hundred years of feminism, from Mary Wollstonecraft and Elizabeth Cady Stanton to Susan B. Anthony, Betty Friedan, and Gloria Steinem, have lost their revered place in our history—their rights overtaken and canceled by the more recent demands of the LGBTQ movement.

Now it is up to us Republicans and conservatives to pick up the fallen banner of feminism.

But the Democrats' flight away from our traditional national goals extends far beyond the realm of social issues, and goes into economics and fiscal policy.

11

The Inflation Nightmare

L ET'S DIG MORE DEEPLY into the inflation issue so we can appreciate how the Democrats are not only forcing up prices, but so debasing our currency in the process, that the dollar is in mortal danger.

It's been almost forty years since America last saw significant inflation. Now, after decades of about 2 percent inflation, we are seeing soaring costs. Gas is up to more than four dollars a gallon. Consumer prices are rising at an annual rate of almost 10 percent.

Democrats live off illusions. The illusion of rising incomes fuels their claims of economic growth and prosperity. But over our shoulders, as we read the Washington economic propaganda, we notice inflation sneaking up behind us, taking away our buying power and eroding our paychecks.

But Washington wants us to believe that's not happening.

Inflation is caused when too much money is seeking to purchase too few goods or services. And boy is Biden deluging the economy with money, at the same time that he is raising taxes and imposing regulations that will tamp down production. Too much money chasing too few goods or services. The excess demand and the limited supply guarantee massive inflation.

Consider how much extra spending Biden wants.

First, he passed a $1.9 trillion spending bill on COVID relief. But now that COVID is ending, he has kept his foot on the gas, raising spending to appease the welfare radicals who elected him.

The economy wants to meet the increased demand with goods and services, but it can't, because it can't find enough new workers.

Who can afford to lose the social welfare programs Biden has passed, by taking a job? When you add up unemployment benefits of $600 per week per person ($62,400 per year for two people), $1,400 per person in stimulus checks, food stamps, Obamacare subsidies, and a tax credit of $3,600 per child, the average family of four, both of whose adults are unemployed, can count on over $100,000 a year in nontaxable income. So who needs a job? Take a job paying $50,000, and lose $100,000 in benefits? No way!

So we now have more than nine million jobs that are going begging. What will happen? Wages—and therefore prices—will have to rise to attract workers, and still shortfalls in production will raise prices even more. Beyond all the Biden spending that is pumping money into the economy, the end of the COVID lockdowns is stimulating demand by letting us out of quarantine so we can go shopping.

Imagine that everybody had their gas tank full of stimulus money but can't drive anyplace because everything's closed. So they sit in the parking garage, waiting for the restrictions to lift. And when they do, all the cars come out at once and cause a massive traffic jam—inflation.

Way too much demand and way too little supply. Inflation. Inflation. Inflation.

Since February 2020, the amount of money sloshing around in American wallets, purses, and checking accounts has shot up by 75 percent—a rise unprecedented in American history—skyrocketing from $3.5 trillion to $6.1 trillion as of May 25, 2021.

This $2.6 trillion of unspent cash is burning a hole in our wallets, even as nine million jobs can't be filled, and inflation goes up by 10 percent a year.

It's called "stagflation." Economic stagnation coming at the same time as inflation.

America was afflicted with stagflation during Jimmy Carter's 1970s. It only ended with Reagan's economic policies in the 1980s.

And here's the dirty little secret the Democrats are keeping quiet about: They *want* inflation. It's not a regrettable byproduct of their policies; it's the *objective*.

Why do the Democrats want inflation?

Inflation lets the Democrats perpetuate the illusion of economic growth and prosperity. Wages are going up. Jobs are plentiful. But it's a mirage. As fast as we make more money, inflation raises the prices we have to pay. So we think we are running ahead, but we are actually just like our pet hamster running on a hamster wheel. The gadget moves backward as fast as the hamster runs forward. He's not running ahead. He's running like hell, but really only running in place.

The Democrats also need inflation in order to pay off the national debt they've racked up.

With our national debt currently at $28.4 trillion, 129 percent of our economy, we owe much more than we produce each year.

It hasn't always been so. This incredible profligacy is a recent development. In 1980, our debt came to only one-third of the size of our economy. Now it is one-third larger!

NATIONAL DEBT AND PERCENT OF GDP BY YEAR		
Year	Debt	Ratio
1960	$286 billion	53%
1970	$371 billion	35%
1980	$908 billion	32%
1990	$3.2 trillion	54%
2000	$5.8 trillion	55%
2010	$13.6 trillion	91%
2020	$28.1 trillion	130%

Forget about paying the debt. That's too wild a dream. We have our hands full just trying to pay the interest and debt service—and even then, we have to borrow more just to do that!

Now, when the Fed is holding interest rates at zero, it's not too onerous. But the Fed says it will begin raising rates by 2023, if not before. With a $28 trillion debt, interest of only 4 percent would require annual appropriation of $1 trillion.

Put that figure into perspective. We now spend $726 billion on defense, $776 billion on Medicare, and $1.2 trillion on Social

Security. So an annual outlay of one trillion dollars—just for interest on the debt—would dwarf defense and Medicare spending. It would almost equal our entire budget for Social Security.

The only way to pay that level of debt service would be out of the same deficit spending that caused it in the first place. We would be borrowing money to pay the interest on what we have already borrowed. It would be just like our pet hamster's treadmill.

Even the crazy liberals and Democrats realize that this is no way to run a country. So what will we do to pay off at least enough of the debt so that the interest payments don't kill us?

There's only one answer: inflation.

Only by a massive increase in prices, and a consequent devaluation of the currency, can we begin to reduce the debt. That process is called *monetizing the debt*, and it is the real Democratic plan. Cheapen the currency. When prices go up, and the value of the dollar, as a consequence, drops, each dollar can buy less than it did before. So you can pay the debt with cheaper money. Nominally, the debt appears to stay the same, but the real purchasing power of the money you use to pay it is much lower.

For example, if you owe $100,000 today and your income is also $100,000 it would take your entire income to pay the debt. But if prices double, and to keep pace, your boss has to double your income, giving you a raise to $200,000, it becomes much easier to pay your debt. It only takes half your income. So the actual amount of your debt stays the same, but the real cost of the debt to you is only half as much. That's how the Democrats plan to pay off the debt: by cheapening the currency.

But think of the damage they do in the process. The price of everything doubles, and your income buys less and less with each paycheck. It makes a mockery of Biden's pledge not to raise taxes on anyone making less than $400,000 a year.

The real purchasing power of everybody's paycheck goes down at the same rate.

One could not imagine anything that would add to the gap between the rich and the poor in America more than inflation. It is the height of cynicism to pretend to give people money and then depreciate the value of that money—and of their existing savings and assets—by inflation. It's the ultimate con game.

But until voters wise up and understand what the liberals are doing to them, it will continue, and even accelerate.

So when the Biden administration says that inflation is under control, what they really mean is that it's going up exactly as they intended, and represents a hidden tax on the poorest of people.

But it can lead to a massive disaster. The end product of devaluing the currency is that people lose faith in paper money. It is just too easy for the government to run the printing press and make more.

The Democrats have made it clear that they do not care about preserving the integrity of our currency, and are willing to debase it through inflation as long as they can give their voters handouts. The fact that these payments increasingly resemble Monopoly money and Confederate currency doesn't matter. Their voters are enthralled by the prospect of more money, even if it becomes increasingly worthless.

In 2020, the value of the dollar shrank by 10 percent, and it is dropping every day. When will people wise up and stop trusting the dollar?

To understand where this is all leading, we need to answer the basic question: what is money?

In Jacob Goldstein's new book, *Money: The True Story of a Made-Up Thing*, he asserts that "money is a made-up thing. A shared fiction." He explains, "Money is fundamentally, unalterably social. The social part of money—the 'shared' in 'shared fiction'—is exactly what makes it money. Otherwise, it's just a chunk of metal or a piece of paper, or in the case of most money today, just a number stored on a bank's computers."[1]

Goldstein explains that "when the pandemic hit . . . central banks could create trillions of dollars, and euros, and yen out of thin air in an effort to fight an economic collapse."[2]

Money has value only because people believe it does. The unspoken transaction that underscores any use of money to buy anything is that "I am giving you this dollar bill because it is worth a certain amount, and you can use it, yourself, to buy that amount of other goods or services."

Once, the dollar and all national currencies were backed by a certain amount of gold on deposit in the central banks of each country. But in 1933, amid a national banking crisis, President Franklin D. Roosevelt closed the gold window to all Americans. No longer could a citizen go to his bank and cash in his dollars for the equivalent amount of metallic gold, although foreigners still could. When other countries followed suit and ended convertibility of their own currencies into gold, money was forever transformed.

In 1973, President Richard Nixon, facing a massive drain on our gold supply due to international demand, took America off the gold standard internationally. Now, not only Americans, but everyone in the world, was precluded from cashing in their currency for gold.

Instead, the dollar—and soon, all other money—became what economists call a "fiat currency" whose value lay only in the pronouncement of the US government that it had a certain worth.

At some level, it was a gigantic bluff that no one called, because the consequences of doing so would be so disastrous and self-immolating that nobody dared to do it.

Except for the Organization of Petroleum Exporting Countries (OPEC). OPEC's sheiks, wise Arab traders, were not about to sell their black gold for pieces of paper printed by foreign governments. They couldn't demand gold anymore, so they raised the price of their oil, in dollars, to keep pace with the erosion of the value of printed currency.

We all saw gas prices soar in the 1970s, but it was an illusion. What was no illusion was the daily impact of inflation in the late 1970s and early 1980s. Supermarkets had to change prices several times each week to keep pace.

After a while, they stopped trying. In the mid-1970s, manual price labels were replaced by electronic bar codes that were scanned at checkout counters. Now, prices could be raised instantly, store-wide, without having to send clerks scurrying around the shelves manually changing them.

The stores said it improved their productivity and reduced errors, but the real reason for the switch was to raise prices so nobody noticed, day after day, week after week.

Gas prices rose when Nixon ended the gold standard in 1973. The dollar lost almost as much purchasing power as gas went up in price. While gas costs rose from $0.39 per gallon, before Nixon ended the gold standard, to $0.55 the next year, the dollar's purchasing power to buy gold fell. Before gas prices rose, it took $66 to buy an ounce of gold. Afterward, it cost $115.

Gas prices didn't really rise so much as the dollar fell. Like a passenger in a car, the scenery seemed to be whizzing by, but in reality it was the car that was moving, not the trees.

In 1947, dimes were made of pure silver, and a gallon of gas cost a dime. Today, while dimes are no longer made of silver, if they were, that amount of silver would still be enough to buy a gallon of gas!

So the value of the dollar—and every other currency—is really an opinion, a consensus of the world's markets.

What could happen if the consensus breaks down and people call the system's bluff? Already, we see signs of this radical change. Gold and silver sales are way up. Crypto-currencies, like bitcoin, are increasing in value as they are more widely used.

People realize that only God can make gold or silver, the government can't. So they come to trust its integrity.

And what is bitcoin but the privatization of money? Distrusting government printed paper bills, people impute a value to a mathematical formula and use it as a form of barter to exchange assets.

The end products of these processes could be catastrophic. Centuries of experience have taught us the perils of letting the free market reign with no government control or regulation. It's like running a nuclear reactor without control rods. Consult those victimized by the Great Depression if you want an example. We have since built an elaborate edifice of controls on the market system to ensure that a crash like that won't happen again. But the big-government liberals have perverted that system to be able to borrow massively and pay the debt back with inflated currencies. The resulting loss of faith in government currency is bringing about a totally unregulated economy, subject to boom and bust cycles that can curl your hair. The wild west returns. Take shelter.

That's what happened in Weimar Germany between the wars. Inflation so depreciated the value of currency that all savings were wiped out and the Hitler/Nazi revolution came to control the country. We can't let that happen here.

12

Free Speech Is Vanishing

Bᴜᴛ ɪᴛ ɪs ɴᴏᴛ only on the economic front that the Left and the Democrats are making America difficult to recognize. They are restricting our basic freedoms—what makes America, America.

Say what you will about the Trump administration, but there was no attempt to muzzle free speech. Trump would out-debate his opponents and even out-shout them, but he never, ever tried to keep them from speaking.

Only the Left and the Democrats do that.

Consider the ways they are attempting to rein in our free speech, and then ponder what they'd do with just one more vote in the Senate.

The Big Tech allies of the Democrats have refused to let Donald Trump, even when he was president of the United States, use Twitter or Facebook to communicate with the country—by censoring, flagging, and then by outright banning.

During his presidency, they claimed that his comments were so inaccurate, and even dangerous, that he was a public menace they could not responsibly permit to use their organs to speak out, putting him in the same category as pornographers and terrorists.

But most of the time, Trump wasn't being inflammatory or dangerous; he was just telling the truth.

- Trump insisted that the COVID virus was leaked to the general public from the Wuhan Institute of Virology, while Beijing insisted it came from a bat. The issue is still unresolved, but most observers now believe Trump was right.
- The media claimed that when Trump crossed Lafayette Park in Washington to speak out in front of St. John's Church, he deliberately walked through the area in which a demonstration was underway, causing injury to the participants. But subsequent reports show that the Secret Service said that the path was clear of demonstrators and nobody was hurt.
- After the January 6 Capitol riot, the media claimed that a Capitol police officer was killed in the melee when he was struck over the head with a fire extinguisher. Pelosi even ordered that his body lie in state underneath the Capitol Rotunda to draw attention to the violence. But the autopsy revealed that he died of a stroke that had nothing to do with the riot.
- Trump was universally mocked in the media for saying that an antimalaria drug, hydroxychloroquine, was an effective treatment for COVID. He has been proven right.

- Trump said there was no evidence he had colluded with Russia to win the 2016 election. After years of investigation, special counsel Robert Mueller came to the same conclusion.
- *The Washington Post* reported that Trump had ordered Georgia election officials to "find evidence of fraud in the 2020 election." Then *The Post* published a correction based on a recording of the call showing that *The Post* had "misquoted Trump's comment on the call."[1]

Based on these alleged Trump "lies," Twitter blocked the president's account.

Three weeks before Election Day in 2020, credible evidence emerged that Joe Biden's son Hunter had brought a laptop in for repair to a Wilmington, Delaware, computer store. On the laptop was clear evidence that the then-vice-president was complicit in receiving questionable payments from the Chinese Communist Party and government. Its contents also established that Biden had lied when he disclaimed any involvement in— or even knowledge of—his son's work for an allegedly corrupt Ukraine energy company, Burisma. Biden's defenders claimed that the computer did not belong to Hunter but had been placed there by Russian intelligence to spread disinformation injurious to Biden.

After President Obama named Vice President Biden as his point man in dealing with Ukraine, Burisma hired Hunter to sit on its board, at a salary of more than $80,000 a month. Hunter's laptop included emails between himself and officials, with him confirming that they'd had dinner with the vice president at his son's behest, presumably to cloak their corruption and to justify their payments to his wayward son.

The laptop even implicated Joe Biden personally. In one of his emails to a co-conspirator, Hunter said he wanted to reserve part of the payout for "the big guy."

Despite the massive national security implications of the scandal, the news was blacked out by the networks and the major newspapers until they were forced to cover it because President Trump raised the issue in a nationally televised debate.

The high-tech outlets even blacked out coverage by the *New York Post*, the ninth largest daily newspaper in the country, because it covered the story.

Hunter admitted that the laptop in question might well be his. The *Daily Mail* examined the laptop and its 103,000 text messages, 154,000 emails, and more than 2,000 photos and videos. The newspaper hired cyber-forensic expert Maryman & Associates, a California firm, to authenticate the laptop. The *Mail* reported that Maryman "matched contents of the laptop with email addresses, contents from an iPad, and an iPhone serial number connected to Biden.["][2]

Quizzed in depth about the provenance of the computer, Hunter was evasive, saying, "For real, I don't know. I really don't know what the answer is. That's the truthful answer."[3]

The director of national intelligence, John Ratcliffe, insisted during the campaign that there is no evidence that the Russians or other foreign actors were behind the emails allegedly found on a laptop linked to Hunter Biden. "Let me be clear," he said. "The intelligence community doesn't believe that, because there is no intelligence that supports that."[4]

Anyone looking at the absence of free speech, the consequences of speaking one's mind, and the attempts to censor and blackball those who disagree with the leftist establishment would never believe that this is indeed happening in the United States of America.

But now, censorship is the norm. Major news stories are blacked out, even by the three mainstream television networks, and reputable journalistic organs such as *The New York Times* and *The Washington Post*. No longer do the censors hide in shame, but boldly proclaim their censorship as being in the national interest.

They refuse to cover former president Donald Trump, and justify their blackout in the name of public safety. Because some of his supporters vented their rage at the US Capitol on January 6, 2021, they take the position that letting America read what its former president has to say could so inflame our citizenry as to constitute a public safety hazard. That is a pretty big muzzle to try to impose on a man that 75 million of us voted to re-elect.

The Facebook panel of censors has condemned our former president to a two-year sentence during which the tech site will not permit his words to reach its users.

Mandatory minimum sentences apparently apply to ex-presidents, even as we repeal them for violent felons.

"Public safety" is the exact same rationale the French revolutionaries used to justify the mass beheadings of political opponents in the 1790s Reign of Terror that was ordered by their Committee on Public Safety. Now the cause of safety is once again condemning our former leaders to silence, albeit while letting them keep their heads (as long as they don't open their mouths).

Presidents' every word and movement used to be covered by a news-hungry media. But in 2020, President Trump found his speeches routinely ignored by most of the media. We had become used to biased coverage, but now we have no coverage of anything with which the media disagrees.

Chris Hughes, co-founder of Facebook, put it best: "The most problematic aspect of Facebook's power is Mark Zuckerberg's control over speech. There is no precedent for his ability to monitor, organize, and even censor two billion people."

The 2020 election coverage by *The New York Times* and *The Washington Post* bore a strong resemblance to that of *Pravda* during Russian elections.

Even when diligent voters successfully hunted out news stories blacked out by the major media organs, they were not permitted to use the Internet to share their knowledge with other voters. Instead, Facebook, Google, Twitter, and others deleted information they didn't like, or opinions with which they disagreed.

Google's search engines featured anti-Trump stories at the top of the page. If you asked Google to tell you about a Trump ad during the campaign, you got four or five pages of derogatory "fact-checking" of its text before Google let you see or read the ad itself. Websites that offered pro-Trump information were blacklisted in the media. Book publishers refused to let their manuscripts see the light of day. Newspapers dropped pro-Trump columnists, whose every utterance they saw as false or even subversive. Not since the McCarthy era in the 1950s has speech been so punished and so roughly censored.

Missouri's Senator Josh Hawley, a Republican, found his new book, *The Tyranny of Big Tech*, dropped by publisher Simon & Schuster because of his alleged role in the January 6th riot. The firm said that it had acted after "witnessing the disturbing, deadly insurrection that took place yesterday in Washington, D.C."[5]

Hawley, whose book was ultimately published by Regnery Publishing, called Simon & Schuster's action "Orwellian." He said that Simon & Schuster's decision not to publish—after originally agreeing to do so—was "a direct assault on the First Amendment. Only approved speech can now be published. This is the Left looking to cancel everyone they don't approve of."[6]

Not only are individual writers or speakers blacklisted, but the Left is trying to sideline entire media networks. In February 2020, the House of Representatives—in the United States, not in Russia—held a hearing on whether the Newsmax television network should be banned from tens of millions of homes. Its sin? Covering the remarks of the president of the United States on the electoral process we had just been through.

In 1933, seeking to consolidate his hold on power, Adolf Hitler used a fire in the Reichstag building—the German Capitol—to justify massive crackdowns, indictments, and even prison sentences.

Things came to a head on January 6, 2021, when unruly and often violent, demonstrators broke into US Capitol, harassing members of Congress. Democrats used this outrageous conduct to justify massive media crackdowns. Anyone who, however obliquely, defended their conduct was seen as subversive. The conduct of the January 6 mob was clearly heinous, but scarcely the attempt at insurrection that the media reported.

"Machine Learning Fairness:" How Big Tech Censors the News

At the intersection of Critical Race Theory and artificial intelligence (AI), we find a computer program called Machine Learning Fairness. Developed at Stanford University in 2014, the program is designed to permit high-tech Internet censors to troll through a vast volume of material to determine what is racist and what is not. It would take manual censors, with their red pencils, months to plow through the mass of material Media Learning Fairness examines every day.

Using AI, programmers feed millions of words and data points into computers to teach them what is acceptable material and what should be blackballed as racist. Big Tech then uses the algorithm to decide what we may read and what must be banned. It's like training your watch dog to bark at strangers.

How can Big Tech get away with such censorship? Oddly, it cites freedom of speech as grounds for censoring speech—a twist that would have made George Orwell proud. Big Tech says that, as a private company, it can say and do what it likes, and censor whom it pleases.

But antitrust law designates certain companies, particularly in transportation, as "common carriers." A common carrier offers its services to the general public under license from a regulatory body. A common carrier holds itself out to provide service to the general public without discrimination for the "public convenience and necessity."[7]

So the Internet could be said to be not just a private company, but also a common carrier.

In 1996, just as the Internet began to catch on, Congress went to the tech companies and said, "Why don't you use this marvelous tool to keep the public informed about political news and opinion?"

Big Tech replied, "We'd love to. But we're worried that if we send out information that is dangerous, like stuff written by terrorists, we could be liable."

"OK," Congress said, "we'll will pass a law giving you immunity for content provided by others, as long as you agree that you won't be biased or discriminate based on party or ideology." Everybody agreed, and the deal was codified in the law as Section 230 of the Communications Decency Act.

But now, Big Tech uses Section 230 as a shield against almost any lawsuits.

The tech companies issue terms-of-service notices to everyone who goes online. Most of us just click "Accept" and pay no attention. The terms explicitly bar tech companies from discriminating based on party or ideology, but these terms of service are almost entirely unenforceable, since Section 230 prevents most lawsuits.

Missouri Republican Senator Josh Hawley argues that Congress should make these terms of service binding, actually enforceable, and require that tech companies apply the terms of service fairly, with no politics bias or discrimination. He says that Congress should pass a law explicitly giving people the right to sue, and imposing a fine of $5,000 per violation.

How to Use the Free Speech Issue to Win

It's not enough to show how biased Big Tech has become, and how it uses its monopoly power to promote its left-wing agenda. To curb these arrogant companies and bring them back to Earth, we must strike directly at their profitable near-monopoly of retail space.

We need to push legislation that is now being sponsored, ironically, by a bipartisan group led by Democratic congresswoman Pramila Jayapal, of Washington, that would break up the Big Tech companies.

The Jayapal bill would force Big Tech companies, like Amazon, to divorce their efforts to sell their own products online, from their informal role as a search engine people can use to find products and services. The evidence suggests that Google is not an impartial search engine listing all possible goods and services for the customer to see and compare. But rather, it puts its thumb on the scale and grants special preference to its own offerings.

Breaking up Google would end its encroaching influence on the entire retail sector, and politically, it would send a shot across its corporate bow to make it rethink its partisanship and bias against the Republican Party and its candidates.

The act of breaking up the Big Tech monoliths would foster competition and curb their arrogant intentions and pretensions.

Senator Hawley also bridles at the way the tech companies use our data to market to us. Every time we do anything online, our Big Tech Big Brothers are watching. They sell this information to advertisers, who use it to figure out how to induce us to buy their stuff.

Have you searched "Paris" or "France" on Google lately? All of a sudden, your computer screen will light up with promotions, offers, references, airlines, hotels, and names of merchants selling trips to France.

Once, Eileen and I were talking to each other about getting a dog. Immediately, ads for dog food, dog trainers, dog boarders, and such showed up on our smart devices.

Hawley proposes Do Not Track legislation to let consumers click a link and bar the collection, distribution, or sale of personal information, purchases, searches, and market data derived from our online interactions.

He also wants to break up the growing Google monopoly that now dominates 90 percent of all searches and 93 percent of the hours spent online in the world.

At a minimum, Google should be forced to give up YouTube, as well as its control of the digital advertising market. Facebook should lose Instagram and WhatsApp—purchases it made for the purpose of forestalling competition.

Amazon has spread its tentacles all over and owns scores of companies providing videos, cloud data collection, drone delivery services, TV and telephone services, a game-streaming company, a satellite communications company, and an online health information service.

Big Tech is the poster boy for the kind of mergers and acquisitions the antitrust laws are supposed to block.

It's time the Republican Party used its political muscle to rein in Big Tech before it totally controls our commercial and political life.

13

Democrats Declare War on Small Businesses

ARE YOU SELF-EMPLOYED, OR a consultant or a freelancer? Do you like being your own boss? Would you like to be your own boss someday?

A third of all American workers now work for themselves or for someone who does. During the COVID lockdown, a lot of us became freelancers. Many got flexible work hours that made it possible for parents to work. Half of all freelancers are caregivers, and freelancing helps them to take care of a child or a parent, often one with disabilities. Some freelancers can choose who they want to take on as clients and what work they want to do. And as their own boss, they can pay themselves whatever they can afford. Two-thirds report making more money than they did when they worked for a company. In a word: they have freedom.

But now the Democrats want to take away that freedom by passing the PRO act. It's one of those Democratic bills whose title implies that it would do the opposite of what it will really do.

PRO stands for "Protecting the Right to Organize." But what it would really do is to force everyone to join a labor union. And because so many of us don't even work for big companies anymore, the PRO Act forces all of us to work for big corporations or companies, and then, to unionize.

So if you work for yourself or for a small company, you would have to give up your job and merge into a big company, or face severe financial penalties. No more sole proprietorships, freelancers, or mom-and-pop operations.

The PRO Act would ban most self-employment and make people go on a payroll. If the PRO Act passes, any business that hires someone part-time or by the project would face heavy fines. You'd have no choice: sign onto a company payroll, or don't work.

The goal is to eliminate the so-called gig economy. Uber and Lyft drivers, for example, would no longer work for themselves. Franchisees would have to close down and become direct employees of the parent company. Writers and bloggers, computer programmers and technicians, food and grocery delivery drivers—even the guy who brings the pizza—many truckers, in-home caregivers, and even babysitters would all have to close down and go to work for a company.

And many of these part-time freelancers would find themselves out of work entirely. Companies that hire them as consultants or part-timers might balk at putting them on payroll. They don't want to have to pay for their FICA, workers comp, unemployment insurance, or have to pay for family leave, especially not for people who only work part-time.

And Congress may soon require them to pay for their health care. It's enough to make any potential employer run screaming.

For the freelancers who have to sign on with a company, they would suddenly find taxes, FICA, unemployment insurance, and workers comp being withheld from their paychecks. All the bureaucratic rules and labor force regulations would suddenly apply to them. And most would have to scale back their fees to fit into the corporate compensation structure.

There are twenty-two million sole proprietorships in the United States today—meaning that they have no employees other than the owner.

The Democratic Party wants to penalize them, and legislation to do so has already passed the House and is pending in the Senate. Biden has pledged to sign it.

The agenda of the Democratic Party—and it's controlling left-wing unions—calls for the elimination of individual entre-preneurship and demands that we all be forced onto company payrolls, there to be regimented and herded into unions whose dues fund their party.

On March 9, 2021, The House passed the PRO Act on a party line vote of 225–206. The unions have made this dangerous piece of legislation their highest priority for the Biden Administration.

The predecessor of the PRO act is already in force in California—called AB 5. It passed the California legislature in 2019, and is killing individual entrepreneur business there.

Americans for Prosperity outlines its major provisions:

- It attempts to push most independent contractors, gig work-ers, and freelancers out of their self-employment and force them into traditional employment arrangements under the National Labor Relations Board (NLRB).

- It forbids businesses from hiring many kinds of independent contractors.
- It eliminates the right-to-work laws in twenty-seven states, including those that have embedded them in their state constitutions.
- It forces employers to hand over the personal information of their employees—including email addresses and cell phone numbers—to union organizers.[1]

The bill even goes so far as to provide that the NLRB need not hold a union election to ask the workers if they want a union. The mere act of getting a majority of the workers to sign cards requesting an election is enough to force a union. (Bear in mind that one-third of the time, when workers request an election, it goes against the union).

Right now, the law allows you to be self-employed if you fit into one of these three categories:

1. You carry on a trade or business as a sole proprietor or an independent contractor. Or,
2. You're in a partnership that does that. Or,
3. You're in business for yourself.

But the PRO Act junks all that. Instead, it says that you can't be considered self-employed by the IRS unless the work you do as a freelancer or consultant is outside the usual business of the company that hires you.

Take a video producer. He couldn't be self-employed if he contracts with a video company to produce videos. He might qualify as self-employed if he cleans their floors, but not if he produces videos.

Why are the Democrats doing this? One reason, and one reason only: to classify people as employees so we can be forced to join unions. Unions that finance their campaigns. The PRO Act basically forces you onto a payroll, and then likely, into a union.

The PRO Act would make anyone who works for a company join its union. No union, no job.

And when a company has no union, the new law would make it easier to force workers to form one. No secret ballot. Snap elections so management doesn't have time to make its case. Rules that stack the elections in favor of the unions. We've seen that happening already.

One of the key changes the New Deal brought was that workers got the right to decide for themselves, free of coercion, whether or not to form a labor union. The National Labor Relations Board holds elections among the workers if enough of them check off cards asking for one.

But the PRO Act eliminates the American-style election and replaces it with a Russian-style one. If a majority of workers sign cards saying they want an election to consider joining a union, Poof! The union is formed! Automatically! And you have to pay union dues, or quit your job. No election. No debate. No time to consider it. No ability to hear competing proposals. And no secret ballot. You're presented with a card to check off while your co-worker, your union organizer, or your best friend is standing right over you, watching.

Is there coercion? Well, judge for yourself. In one-third of the cases where a majority of workers sign cards asking for a union election, the union loses in the subsequent voting. After the workers who checked off the card think about it, outside of the glare of their union representative, they give a thumbs down.

So the unions came up with the PRO Act to eliminate the inconvenience of even holding an election. No choice; just sign here.

Why not form a union?

Well, first of all, the union bosses take a lot better care of themselves than they do of their workers. Every year, union officials, administrators, leaders, and organizers pay themselves $1.1 billion. But the workers in their unions get only $2.5 billion. More than a quarter of the money goes to the union bosses, not to the workers. In fact, there have been 2,056 racketeering indictments against unions since 2000.

That's the cesspool the PRO Act holds in store for each of us who now is happily self-employed. We would go from working for ourselves, to working for a company, to having to join a union. Like it or not.

Fall of Union Membership

Why are the unions pressing so hard for the PRO Act? Because they are desperate. The percentage of Americans in labor unions has declined every year since 1980. At the moment, only 14.3 million people are in unions—a mere 10.8 percent of the labor force. Back in 1983, 20.1 percent of the labor force was unionized. Now it's only half that.

While private sector unionization has been dropping steadily, public sector unions grew. The reason was simple: private sector unions faced competition from non-union companies at home and abroad, while public sector unions legislated themselves monopoly status through contracts with Democratic governors in blue states. Between 2000 and 2019, private sector union membership fell from 9 percent to 6.2 percent of the labor force. Now, the public employee unions are dominant. A majority of unionized workers are employed by the federal, state, or local government. Meanwhile, private sector union bosses got the message: like dinosaurs, they were dying out.

Their first response was to force people to join unions as a precondition of employment, so twenty-seven states passed right to work laws that prohibited that. Now they're trying get rid of the right to work laws through the PRO Act.

The unions don't seem to accept that the composition of the labor force is changing.

Rise of Sole Proprietorships

The 22 million sole proprietorships operating in the United States are fragile. Twenty percent don't survive their first year—and only 70 percent are still around after two years, according to the Small Business Administration (SBA). Five years later, only half are still afloat.

But they are a hardy bunch. The American entrepreneurial impulse is hard to kill. Like covered wagons going west 150 years ago, 400,000 new sole proprietorships try their skill and luck every year.

They face all kinds of hardships in gaining market share, acquiring public recognition, getting financing, building their reputation, and establishing themselves. But through pluck, energy, and luck, most are making it. But the one thing they cannot overcome is the PRO Act.

There are lots of reasons to vote Republican this year. But if you are in business for yourself, or employing only your family, there is one especially compelling reason: survival! The Democrats, simply put, want to make your business illegal.

Forced Unionization as an Issue in 2022 and 2024

So far, the crazy leftists that run the Democratic Party have had the good sense not to try to pass the PRO Act in the Senate, even after it passed the House earlier this year.

The popular backlash against it would be intense. It would immediately mobilize 22 million people who work for themselves and do not want to have a boss.

Because this terrible bill has already passed the House, with the support of 235 Democratic Congressmen, it can be a key element in our strategy to retake the chamber.

Republicans need to get lists, in each district, of sole proprietorship businesses, and via phone, mail, and email, reach out to alert them to the danger of the PRO Act, and to its potential impact on their lives and businesses.

With the on-the-record votes of all 235 Democrats (each of whom is running for re-election in 2022) this issue could be key to sending Nancy Pelosi back home to San Francisco.

14

China Takes Over: It's Not Independence Day

I N MANY WAYS, PATRIOTISM has never been stronger in the United States, but we must all have the creeping feeling inside that we are becoming China's colony, or at least it's patsy.

President Donald Trump had gone a long way to make us independent, but Biden has undone much of his good work.

We were, after fifty years of trying, finally energy independent. In 2020, for the first time in sixty-two years, we sold more oil abroad than we imported. Our production rose 11 percent, and consumption fell by 1 percent in the past year alone.

But then Biden struck, restricting fracking (horizontal drilling), limiting off-shore oil production, stopping Arctic drilling, and ending all tax credits for energy production. While he claimed that his policies reduced carbon emissions to help stop global climate change, he did nothing to stop China from building all the coal plants it wants. So worldwide emissions of carbon have risen, even as the United States has cut its fossil fuels drastically. As we were cutting our coal production, China doubled its fossil fuel output.

China now emits more carbon than the rest of the developed world combined! Beijing accounts for 27 percent of the world's emissions. If carbon pollution were a crime, China would be the leading suspect. By contrast, the United States now accounts for only 11 percent of global emissions. Japan emits only 4 percent, and Europe 10 percent. India belches out 7 percent of the globe's total. China is the carbon culprit!

Chinese propagandists point out that while China emits more than twice America's carbon, it is far lower in its per capita output, given its huge population of 1.412 billion. But they fail to explain India, which, with slightly fewer people—1.379 billion—emits only a quarter as much carbon as China does. China's carbon emissions are a form of fossil fuel imperialism.

When President Trump refused to sign the Paris Climate Accords in 2016, he cited China's failure to abide by its limits. Indeed, when China—to global applause and praise from its sycophants abroad—announced that it was going to limit its emissions, it was, in reality, only agreeing to begin cutting them by 2033!

And it's not just energy. China's encroachments on American independence have become legion. Forbes writes that "over 70 percent of active pharmaceutical ingredients used in the U.S. market are produced overseas. Almost all of the ibuprofen sold here comes from China."[1]

China became the major player in global technology. Most telecom equipment is made in China. It has become the leading supplier of 5G equipment. The largest owner of patents is the Chinese-owned company Huawei, with ties to the Beijing military that is effectively controlled by the government that has become a poster child of Chinese technology.

How did China amass such power? We gave it to them. We were the "useful idiots"[2] Lenin said would facilitate the growth of communism and the demise of capitalism.

A recent study found that the United States is now dependent on foreign suppliers and producers for not only cheap components and consumer goods like sneakers and plug-in headphones, but also high-end electronics, major pharmaceutical inputs and medical equipment, and also defense supplies and technology.

Biden says that his infrastructure initiatives will permit us to "own the future."[3] He wants to build half a million charging stations on our highways for electric cars. He proposes wind energy turbines that will dot the landscape, generating power. He wants a big investment in solar energy. Renewable resources, he says, are the future.

But he forgot one little thing. To operate the electric batteries for his cars, the solar panels, and the windmills all require what are called "rare earth" minerals. And we don't have any.

We have to import almost $200 million of rare earth minerals a year, and 80 percent come from guess where? China.

There are seventeen rare earth minerals, valuable because of they are strongly magnetic and great conductors of electricity. You probably haven't heard of any of them. I know I hadn't. They have names like Lanthanum, Lutetium, and Europium. Names only a chemistry set could love.

But we'll have no trouble recognizing the products they—and only they—can power: computers, smartphones, jet engines, lasers, satellites, fiber optics, DVD players, televisions, and missile guidance systems.

They also power those little electric car batteries Biden wants to charge, and the solar panels he wants to erect so we can own the future.

We don't mine or process much in the way of rare earth metals. So when you talk of charging stations for electric cars before you've got the rare earth minerals to make the batteries . . . well, pardon me, but you're putting the cart before the horse. And when you want to build your wind turbines without rare earth metals, you're just tilting at windmills, like Don Quixote did.

We used to have a global monopoly of rare earth minerals. Until 1980, we mined and processed 99 percent of the world's rare earth minerals. Now China produces ten times as many rare earth minerals as we do.

What happened? How did we lose our edge in these vital minerals?

Private companies were doing fine by mining and refining them. But in 1980, the globalists, the environmentalists, and the government regulators stepped in and put them all out of business. It began when the International Atomic Energy Agency (IAEA)—the same guys who are letting Iran get nuclear weapons—decided to start regulating rare earth minerals, most of which were mined as byproducts of uranium and thorium. There was no good reason to regulate them; they can't be turned into nuclear weapons. But the IAEA couldn't keep its hands off them.

Suddenly, the American rare earth mineral industry found itself saddled with extensive licensing, regulatory, disposal, and liability rules. The extra costs drove them out of business, one after the other.

China, meanwhile, didn't give a damn what the IAEA said. It wasn't even a member. Beijing flat-out refused to pay any attention to their regs. So while we had to close our mines, they were busy opening theirs.

And under the trade agreements Bill Clinton negotiated with China, American companies lined up to mine China's rare earth minerals, bringing with them the mining and refining technologies that China was happy to steal. Useful idiots! Entire US industries, like medical imaging, picked up and moved to China.

And then the Pentagon compounded the problem. A misguided regulation required US defense contractors to use only alloys produced in America. But while the alloys are made here, the rare earth minerals on which they are based all come from China. So the regulation, designed to keep production in American hands, really ensured China's continued dominance.

Then, thank God Donald Trump stepped in.

In 2019, he amended the law so it would be based on where the minerals were mined, not where the alloys were manufactured. So the Pentagon could no longer use Chinese rare earth minerals to produce our weapons and equipment. The Pentagon had to get off its butt and find other sources of rare earth minerals.

Because of Trump's new law, the defense people began to create a market again for American rare earth minerals. In 2019, we increased our domestic production by 44 percent, making us second only to China in production.

And on November 17, 2020, Trump's Department of Defense awarded a $9.6 million grant to MP Materials, the owner of Mountain Pass Mine, the largest rare earth mine in the Western Hemisphere.

But despite Trump's efforts, China is hell-bent on dominating the global rare earth mineral market. Then they can, as poor, demented Joe Biden said, "control the future." They are going around, building roads and other goodies for African countries, in return for exclusive rights to mine their minerals. Russell Parman, a foreign intelligence officer with the US Army Aviation and Missile Command, reports that China is targeting "Cameroon, Angola, Tanzania, and Zambia." He adds, "Tanzania is of particular interest because of the presence of several military-critical rare earths, which are key components in precision-guided munition technology."

For now, China still has the dominant market share of rare earth minerals, and boy does it know how to use it.

In 2010, Japan and China quarreled over some offshore islands. China retaliated by cutting off rare earth mineral exports to Japan. Tokyo folded like a cheap suit.

Listen to what the Communist Party newspaper, the *People's Daily*, had to say about China's leverage over us:

> At present, the United States completely overestimates its ability to control the global supply chain and is due to slap itself in the face when it sobers up from its happy, ignorant self-indulgence.

Indeed.

So when Joe Biden lays on all his dreams of electric cars recharging on the highway, windmills turning and generating electricity, and solar panels heating up to produce power, he's just in a fantasy world of his own.

The only way to do that at present is to put ourselves totally at the mercy of the Chinese Communist Party.

Hey, we didn't struggle for fifty years to get out from under Arab domination of our oil to put ourselves under Chinese control, just because our president wants to get some votes by fighting global warming.

I'm not against electric cars, windmills, or solar energy. But first, develop our rare earth mineral industry so we can be self-sufficient. Don't go throwing away our whole car industry and our oil and gas companies to convert to electric cars, solar, and wind until we produce the necessary minerals right here at home.

In the 1890s, China fought a war with Britain to try to stop London from selling opium to the Chinese people. It was called the Opium War. The poor people in China were getting hooked, and the Chinese government wanted to stop it. Now we have to stand up and wean ourselves of our addiction to Chinese rare earth minerals. Once we do, you can have all the electric cars you want. But first things first.

China's Plan for Us

China's increasing power *vis-à-vis* the United States is troubling, particularly when we consider the plans Beijing has in store for us.

Empires of the past were constructed around military power. Ideology didn't matter. Roman legions just marched into country after country and took over.

As the Middle Ages dawned, and the Renaissance loomed, empires were increasingly built on religion. The Western world was divided between Roman Catholic and Protestant territory. As nation-states began to emerge, nationalism provided the structure around which empires were built. With the coming of the Industrial Revolution, and into the twentieth century, economics was the basis for empire as capitalism and Marxism divided the world between them.

But China's strategy for global domination is not hinged on nationalism or ideology. It is based on the concept of mind control made possible by our electronic information system.

China maintains its power over its own vast population by using the Internet to manipulate the flow of information on the one hand, and to track down dissenters and dissidents on the other.

The regime formulates a "social acceptance score" for each person—rather like a credit rating. The score is based on spying and probing into everything each of us says or writes. Those whose outward actions and innermost thoughts bespeak loyalty to the regime are rewarded by high social scores.

And scores matter. They can determine what kind of job you get and how much you get paid. Those who have the audacity to think for themselves—and the incompetence not to be able to fully hide it—find it hard to get on passenger airplanes or trains, rent or buy good housing, find a good job, or be accepted into society. It is George Orwell's dystopian world outlined in his book *1984*, brought to life.

China's efforts are particularly focused on spreading the domination of its effectively government-controlled company Huawei, in the market for 5G information systems. With Huawei software systems embedded in the world's computers, China will be able to monitor our most confidential communications. Whether you live in New York or Beijing, the Chinese Communist Party will be able to eavesdrop on what you write, say, and increasingly, think.

We will eventually each have our individual social acceptance score, amassed according to standards and opinions of our masters in China.

China's economic clout is both enormous and growing rapidly. With a communist economy, the public and private sectors are commingled to create a global powerhouse.

In 2008, China's major companies ranked a collective sixth in the world, with $1.1 trillion in assets. By 2020, they ranked second only to the United States, with $8.3 trillion. (The United States is barely ahead, with $9.8 trillion.) In 2008, none of the Chinese companies was even in the top ten.[4] Now, three of the top five companies in the world are Chinese.

Consider the scope of China's control over the American economy. Fox News' Hollie McKay writes that China "produces 97 percent of U.S. antibiotics and about 90 percent of active pharmaceutical ingredients" in US medicines. She continues: "Chinese firms have bought AMC Entertainment, Legendary Entertainment, and other media companies. Control of 8,000-plus of American theater screens and other media platforms allows China to project 'soft power' and block unflattering depictions of the Chinese government from being presented, both in terms of creative production and mass distribution."[5]

The American Security Institute reports that Chinese firms and investors "own a controlling majority in nearly 2,400 American companies."[6] This list includes AMC Entertainment (entertainment), Cirrus Wind Energy (energy), Complete Genomics (health care), First International Oil (energy), G.E. Appliances (technology), IBM–P.C. division (technology), Motorola Mobility (technology), Nexteer Automotive (automotive), Riot Games (entertainment), Smithfield Foods (food), Teledyne Continental Motors and Mattituck Services (aerospace), Terex Corp. (machinery), Triple H Coal (mining), Zonare Medical Systems (health care).[7]

We can foresee the day when China's massive economic power—given it by American dependence on Chinese products and services—can be used to curtail the commercial and business opportunities of those who are politically unreliable. Our social acceptance score—as measured by the new Mandarins in China—could directly govern whether we get a good job or a promotion, get our books published, or receive favorable coverage on social media or from news organs.

Chinese companies have focused on targeted acquisitions to access confidential information about Americans. US regulators killed Chinese private equity firm Orient Hontai's proposed $1.4 billion acquisition of American marketing firm AppLovin over concerns about data security under a foreign owner.[8]

Once again, President Donald Trump has come to our rescue. He, in effect, declared war on the Huawei company, imposing sanctions on them, limiting their capacity to access the chips vital to their business. Trump led the way in cracking down on Chinese stealing of our intellectual property. In 2018, his administration indicted Meng Wanzhou, a senior Huawei executive and the daughter of the company's founder. She was arrested in Canada, accused of lying to banks about Huawei's relationship with its Iran-based affiliate. She was also accused of plotting to steal the trade secrets and intellectual property of rival companies in the United States.

Then, inexplicably, Biden let Meng go free after his justice department agreed to suspend the fraud charges against her. Biden's rank appeasement of China stands in sharp contrast to Trump's vigilance in protecting our interests. Huawei's efforts to steal our IP went very far.

ABC News reported that prosecutors said, "Huawei recruited employees of competitors to steal intellectual property. The company also provided incentives to its own employees by offering bonuses to those who brought in the most valuable stolen information, and it used proxies, including professors at research institutions, in the pursuit of inside information. The stolen information included antenna and robot testing technology, as well as user manuals for Internet routers. One goal of the theft," the Department of Justice said, "was to allow Huawei to save on research and development costs."[9]

The administration's sanctions against Huawei are bearing fruit. The malign corporation has fallen from number one to number nine in the world in 5G technology. Trump crippled Huawei's technological dominance by severely limiting its ability to use American technology to design and manufacture semiconductors produced for it abroad. Now, the company is emphasizing sales of electric cars, as opposed to the high tech 5G iPhones that were once its speciality.

But the key question nags: Why did Biden free Meng? Did it have anything to do with his own dealings with China and the millions he and his son made there?

Biden's Financial Relations with China

The full facts of Joe and Hunter Biden's financial relationship with the Chinese Communist Party may never be fully known.

Attention has focused on Hunter's fabled laptop that was unearthed after it was retrieved from a repair shop in Wilmington. Despite the earnest efforts of the Democrats and their supportive media allies to discredit its veracity and peddle the ridiculous narrative that it was a product of Russian disinformation, the overwhelming evidence is that the laptop is, indeed, genuine.

Hunter Biden's laptop contradicts his father's contention that he had nothing to do with his son's business transactions abroad. *The Wall Street Journal* reports that on the laptop is clear evidence that "the vice president made an 'unscheduled' stop at a private restaurant dinner in April 2015, where Hunter was hosting an official of the Ukrainian gas company Burisma." *The Journal* puts the revelation into perspective: "Understand: If Hunter's role on Burisma's board was to make the company a hot potato for Ukrainian corruption investigators, the vice president's stop-by succeeded instantly in turning the administration's Ukraine policy into a hostage to Burisma, avoiding prosecution."

Nor was the laptop's evidence any less damning when it revealed the true nature of the vice president's involvement with his son's dealings with China.[10]

Peter Schweizer, who earned his spurs investigating the depth of the corruption in the Clinton Foundation, says that "Files in Hunter Biden's laptop confirm that Joe Biden was a 'direct beneficiary' of Hunter Biden's foreign business deals." He predicted that, when all the facts are known, they will "expose disastrous dimensions of Biden family corruption."[11]

Schweizer notes that "we're in the middle of the investigation now, but by the end of the year it will be completed, and it will take on a far more sinister tone than it has, even now, in terms of what it says about the Biden family and the vulnerabilities of the Biden family." He concludes, chillingly, "It's that bad."[12]

The Wall Street Journal sets to rest any doubt about the authenticity of the laptop, writing in a story headlined, "'Hunter Biden's Laptop Is Real: Let the Dam Break.' The New York tabloid's reporting [the *New York Post's*], and that of the *Daily Mail*, which also has the laptop data, is everything journalism aspires to be, based on transparently obtained, contemporaneous documentation, not on somebody's after-the-fact recollection or spin. Their reporting makes the average Bob Woodward book look like the product of Ouija board reporting."[13]

Less publicized, but potentially more damaging, is the $22 million of Chinese money that flowed into the Biden Center for Diplomacy and Global Engagement Institute at the University of Pennsylvania.

In 2017, shortly after leaving office as vice president, Joe Biden launched the Center, with his name on it, through the University of Pennsylvania. The Center functioned as a think tank and home-away-from-home for people who would become top officials in the Biden administration's foreign policy establishment.

Chief among them was Tony Blinken, who served as the managing director of the Center from 2017 to 2019—at a salary of $80,000—before becoming Biden's secretary of state. Biden himself earned nearly $1 million as a professor at the institute in 2018 and 2019. He taught no classes and rarely appeared on campus.

According to the National Legal and Policy Center (NLPC), UPenn received more than $70 million from Chinese sources between 2013 and 2019. Of that amount, about $22 million was logged as coming from anonymous sources in China.

The avalanche of funding started shortly after the Biden Center was officially opened. In May 2018, the largest anonymous donation from China rolled in, totaling $14.5 million. More money was donated once Biden announced he was running for president.

Paul Kamenar, attorney for the NLPC, said that UPenn "isn't coming clean" on the anonymous donations. "Why aren't you releasing this information so we can see who these Chinese sources are and how much money is being funneled to the Biden Center? You have to scratch your head and say, 'What's going on here?' Millions of dollars are being funneled to the Biden Center, and you don't have to be Sherlock Holmes to find out that the Biden Center isn't making its money off bake sales."[14]

So whether channeled through son Hunter, or the University of Pennsylvania, after leaving the vice presidency, Biden has basically made his living working for China.

Nobody ever said Biden was an ingrate. He has nominated the president of the University of Pennsylvania, Amy Guttman, to serve as US Ambassador to Germany.

We have elected a president who was on China's payroll prior taking office.

15

Biden Wants to Take Your Assets

BIDEN HAS COME UP with the ultimate socialist proposal to stop parents from leaving money to their children, to stop mom-and-pop stores from surviving one more generation, and to stop family farms from staying in the family.

Plenty of left-wing presidents have raised the capital gains tax, even as conservatives have lowered it. A tug of war.

But Biden wants to go far beyond raising it. He wants to change it so that it becomes a socialist tool to end inherited wealth, farms, homes, businesses, land, or anything else. No more inheritances. When you die, your kids have to start from scratch. Your savings? Your assets? Your farm? Your home? Most likely gone.

He wants to change totally the very concept of capital gains taxation so that it becomes, not a device to raise revenue, but a way to force owners of small businesses, family farms, and small investors to sell their assets to the government or to large business conglomerates.

It seeks not so much to fund social programs as to punish inheritance and soak the successful.

It is a leveler's tax dream. Robin Hood on steroids.

A capital gains tax is . . . well, a tax on capital gains. You buy your home, farm, store, business, stocks, bonds, or whatever at a certain price, and then you sell at a higher price. The profit is a capital gain, and the government want a share of it through the capital gains tax.

But Biden's capital gains tax is totally different. It's really more of an inheritance tax. And a huge one.

Currently, if you buy your home or farm for $100,000, and its value goes up by $50,000, you don't pay any tax on the added value until you or your heirs sell. But Biden wants to change that, collecting the extra tax when you die, even if you and your heirs don't sell.

Under current law, if your home goes up to $150,000 in value during your lifetime, your son or daughter inherits it at its current value, $150,000. That's called a "stepped-up basis." The heirs do not have to pay capital gains taxes on the extra $50,000 that it gained while your mom and dad owned it. Because they never sold it, there is no tax to pay, and you inherit it at the full $150,000 value. But now, Biden and the government want to hit you with a tax on the extra $50,000 increase in value right after your parents die, even if there was no sale.

The current law says that you don't have to pay a capital gains tax on your land, or your company, or your business, or your farm until you sell it. Makes sense. The only way you make the money is to sell it and then you can cut the government in on your profit.

But Joe Biden and the Democrats won't wait that long. Their new bill will make you pay the tax the moment you die. As your body is hauled out the front door, the tax man comes in the back with his calculator.

He'll want to know how much your parents paid for their house, company, stock, farm, or land, and then how much they could have sold it for had they lived.

But they didn't live. They're dead. They didn't sell it, and neither did you. Doesn't matter. The Biden tax reaches out from the grave and scoops out its take. But you probably don't have the money to pay the tax. If you had sold the house, that would be easy. You'd just give the government a portion of your profit on the sale.

But under the Biden proposal, you owe the money even if you don't sell. So you have to reach into your savings and hope you can come up with enough to pay the government. Otherwise, they'll come in and take away your home, your farm, your business, your pension, your stocks, your bonds. So it's not a tax as much as it is a confiscation, a taking, an eviction.

It doesn't tax capital gains so much as it taxes inheritance. But the politicians don't dare call it an inheritance tax. They have learned their lesson. Talk about inheritance taxes in Washington, and it conjures images of family farms going up for auction, small businesses that can't be passed down. Jilted children and aggrieved widows.

Reagan mobilized opposition to the inheritance tax by calling it the "death tax." Reminds us of what Ben Franklin said are the only two things in life that are certain: death and taxes. So they renamed it—now it's called the capital gains tax. A technical investment tax that only matters to Wall Street.

Hey, President Biden, my mom and dad just died. I lost them. And now you want my house, too? Now? You're kidding me? Right?

If the house lost value, does the government pay you money? No way. Doesn't work like that. It's a capital *gains* tax. Capital loss? That's your problem. You're on your own, buddy.

And who's to say how much the house is worth? If your parents were still alive, it'd be clear. You'd take what you got when they sold it, and subtract what they bought it for. But if you or your parents never sold it, you're just guessing. Lawsuits. Lawyer fees. Kickbacks. Corruption. A real mess.

And how about that gift that keeps on giving? Inflation? What is the $100,000 your folks paid for the house worth today? How much of the $50,000 profit isn't a capital gain at all, but just a way to keep pace with inflation. But you get no credit for inflation. No adjustment.

Its a stacked deck. You pay a tax on the gain, even if there was no gain. And if the property lost value, you get no help.

It's a way to make people pay taxes on money they made on paper long ago but never actually got.

But here's what it really is—an eviction notice. The government knows you haven't got the money to pay the tax—that is, until there is an actual sale. But Biden wants the money right now.

So it's a way to force you to sell. Who benefits? The government? No. You haven't got the money to pay the tax. But a lot of people do make money.

A lot of money. The big agribusiness company that's wanted to buy your dad's farm for fifty years, but he wouldn't sell. Now you'll have to. The big chain store that wants to close your family grocery and open up their brand on the same corner.

The appraiser and accountants who can't wait for the extra business. The stockbroker who wants the commission on the stock you'll have to sell. The real estate mogul and his agent who want to get their hands on your house.

But this is not a tax that is motivated by greed. It's not about greed. It's about envy. Eileen told me about a book thirty years ago by Nancy Friday. It was entitled *Jealousy*.[1] She differentiated between jealousy, which she said was a positive emotion (I want what you have, so I'll work hard to make enough to buy it), and the opposite, envy (I hate that you have all this. I just want you not to have it. I'd rather see you die than have it.).

The Russians tell the story of Ivan, a devout Christian farmer who died in a fire when his house burned down. St. Peter greeted him at the gate and said, "You've led such a virtuous life. Is there anything I can do for you?"

"Yes," Ivan answered. "My neighbor, Boris, I want his house to burn down, too."

And it's no coincidence that this is a Russian story, because communism and wokeism are both based on envy. I hate you for your success and want you to die rather than enjoy it. But American capitalism is based on jealousy. I love your new car. I'd like to own a car like that. So I'll work extra hours or go back to school so I can buy a car just like that.

Capitalism versus Socialism

The woke Left is copying a page from the history of British socialism. Right after World War II, a radical Left Labour Party government took over from Churchill's Conservatives. They nationalized everything they could get their hands on.

A joke by Winston Churchill always cracks me up. Right after the Labour Party leader Clement Attlee defeated him, the two ran into each other in the men's room of the House of Commons. Churchill was standing at a urinal when Atlee entered. Winston abruptly adjusted his jacket for privacy.

"Shy, Winston?" Atlee joked.

"No," Churchill said, in his famous accent. "No, it's not that at all. It's just that whenever you see anything that is big and impressive, you nationalize it!"

When Labour took over in 1946, as the war ended, English envy was at its height. A national housing shortage did not improve the mood of British soldiers and sailors returning home to overcrowded dwellings. Anger and envy against wealthy English families with baronial estates mounted, prompting the Labour government to hike inheritance taxes from 20 percent to 40 percent to 55 percent to 65 percent to 75 percent, before settling in at 85 percent in 1969.

Because the homes, which had been in the aristocratic families for generations (and sometimes for centuries), had never been sold, their new owners had no ready pool of funds to use in paying the taxes when their parents passed away. It was much the same system as the woke Left wants to create here, using the Biden capital gains tax program.

The new heirs couldn't pay the taxes and were forced, en masse, to sell their homes to developers. The resulting demolition of many of the United Kingdom's most beautiful, historic, and architecturally unique homes led to public anger. But rather than let the owners live in their homes by lowering the inheritance tax rate, the government set up the National Land Trust to receive donations of their home in return for tax forgiveness.

Now the radical Left in the United States is showing its true goal: force successful people to suffer, lose their wealth, and be taxed out of their homes, and bar them from passing on to their children the fruits of their own labor.

But for the most part, these are not baronial estates we are talking about. American society is so much more egalitarian than the British class system ever was.

No, these are family farms whose soil their owners have tilled with their own hands for decades. The properties that could be seized are the small mom-and-pop grocery stores that held neighborhoods together. They are the family homesteads to which generations of children repaired every Thanksgiving and Christmas.

And the financial assets are no huge estates symbolizing wealth and privilege. They are the earnings and savings of a lifetime. The pensions accrued after a lifetime of public service protecting citizens or extinguishing fires. They are often all that a middle-class family has left after the factory that they gave their blood, sweat, and tears to for generations closed and moved to China.

Those are the stakes when Biden changes the capital gains tax into a vehicle for confiscation of what the middle class have left after their parents die. The Republicans in Congress have managed to beat back Biden's proposal, for now. But don't be fooled. It remains prominently featured on the Left's agenda to resurface if they ever get their hands on the Senate.

Enter: The Billionaire's Haircut

At this writing, the Senate Democrats are scrambling for revenue sources to pay for trillions in new welfare spending they hope to jam through with only Democratic support. So they have cast their envious eyes on the large fortunes of America's billionaires.

They propose not a tax, but what has come to be known in Europe as a "haircut." A tax is typically levied on income or other earnings. A haircut falls on assets that are just sitting there in your portfolio or bank account. They have, of course, already been taxed, and they are what is left.

But the Left wants another bite at the apple. In fact, an annual bite.

The Democrats propose that the government figure out what your investments, your home, your farm, your house, and your other assets were worth at the start of the year, and what they are worth at the end. Then they want to tax you ten percent of your gain. It's not a capital gains tax that only taxes the gain when you realize it by selling. But a haircut that taxes your capital gain even if you never cashed in and it remains, at most, a theoretical number.

The initial proposal is to tax only billionaires. But these taxes, once passed, have a way of trickling down so that they hit people of more modest means. Look at the Alternative Minimum Tax. It was originally levied on the wealthy who pay little or no taxes. But then, inflation and tax increases made it apply to tens of millions of us.

16

Packing the Country: Immigration and the Latino Vote

FOR ALL THE DISCUSSION of Democratic plans to pack the Supreme Court by adding additional judges, and to pack the Senate by admitting new states, the fact is that Biden is packing the country by adding new voters he thinks will then be loyal to him.

We often have presidents whose humanitarian impulses overrode their common sense and led them to open our borders wide to anyone who wants to come. But Joe Biden is unique. He does not see limitless illegal immigration as a problem—much less a crisis. He sees it as an opportunity to reshape the national electorate.

Long ago, the Democrats gave up on winning elections among our current population. Americans were too wed to traditional values to go along with the claptrap the Left was pushing, so the Left decided to create a new American electorate by adding tens of millions of Hispanics and Latinos, who they confidently felt would be their political puppets.

As the Latino population rose—through a high birth rate, legal immigration, and illicit entry into the United States—it seemed the strategy was working, big time.

HISPANIC POPULATION IN U.S. BY YEAR	
2010	16.4 million
2012	16.9 million
2014	17.3 million
2016	17.8 million
2018	18.3 million
2019	18.5 million

Between 1990 and 2005, the illegal immigrant population in the United States more than tripled.

Then, at the end of the Clinton Administration, as popular reaction mounted to the rising levels of illegal entry, Clinton started to build a Southern border wall that Trump almost completed, and is now being increasingly dismantled by Biden. Between 2005 and the start of the Trump Administration in 2017, the population of illegal immigrants actually dropped by almost one million. Under Trump, it fell further.

But under Biden, all bets are off. The Border Patrol reports that, by May 2021, illegal immigration into the United States had doubled. They have been intercepting an average of 3,500 illegal aliens each day in 2021.

Biden used a variant of the old carrot-and-stick approach to pad the ranks of illegal immigrants. He offered a carrot to come here, legally or not, but he dispensed with the stick by ending any enforcement of the immigration laws.

The carrot he offers is big. He has extended unprecedented benefits to illegal immigrants that are, in effect, incentives to come here illegally and break the law. He offers:

- $1,400 stimulus checks to all illegal immigrants
- Unemployment benefits running to $600 per week, even with no prior history of employment in the country
- Free health care under Medicaid
- In-state reduced tuition at state colleges
- Eligibility for food stamps

He has even paid for families of illegal immigrants already in the United States to fly south to greet the new arrivals at the border.

Tragically, his incentives have impelled children to leave their homes and families to come, with no one to accompany them, to the US border. In March 2021 alone, 19,000 unaccompanied minors came here.

But beyond offering carrots, Biden has ended efforts to catch, deter, or deport illegal immigrants. And in 2021, when tens of thousands of would-be Haitian immigrants clustered under the Del Rio Bridge on the Mexican border, Biden let twelve thousand stay in the United States, doubtless encouraging tens of thousands more to hazard the trip.

He has returned to the dreadful catch-and-release policy on the Southern border. He, in effect, asks American ICE agents to risk their lives apprehending those who cross illegally, only to release them in short order.

By contrast, Trump cut deals with Mexico, guaranteeing that it would hold illegal immigrants on the Mexican side of the border to stop them from entering the United States. Impelled by incentives in the new USMCA (United States-Mexico-Canada Agreement)—and the threat of sanctions—Mexico deployed almost thirty thousand troops to block its citizens, and migrants from other countries, from entering the United States illegally.

The Trump move was designed to circumvent the tactics that leftist lawyers and judges had been using to skirt US immigration laws by filing phony asylum claims. US courts had ruled that illegal immigrants were entitled to the entire panoply of civil and constitutional rights once they set foot on our soil, even if their initial entry to our country was illegal. They were also entitled to free lawyers as they litigated their claims.

In most cases, these asylum applicants were not fleeing political oppression—the traditional grounds for asylum—but claimed their migration was impelled by poverty and crime. Biden has moved to expand the grounds for asylum to accommodate these claims.

The results of the Biden policies are that illegal immigration in May 2021 rose by 700 percent, and more unaccompanied minors had arrived here in early May than in any prior month in our history.

Doesn't one thing begin to dawn on you as you read these facts? Biden and the radical Left not only *do not* want to cut back on immigration enforcement, they want to encourage illegal immigration. They support it. Why? Well, that part's easy. Because they want to use these new Americans to pack the electorate so they can keep winning elections.

Latinos Reject the Woke Left

But it's not working out that way. There is no other way to say it: the Democratic Party goofed! For two decades, Democratic strategists have counted on winning the Latino or Hispanic vote overwhelmingly, establishing dominion over this ethnic group, much as they have done over Jewish and African-American voters. So they have worked overtime to bring more Hispanics into the country, urging open borders and amnesty. They have said Republicans are on the wrong side of history and destined to become extinct.

They saw the future clearly. With Hispanics rising steadily as a proportion of our population, all they had to do was win the Latinos and ride that demographic into permanent power. Indeed, as the Latino proportion of our population soared, now nearing 19 percent (versus 12 percent for Blacks), there seemed to be method to their madness.

So they worked passionately to bring more Hispanics into the country, urging open borders and amnesty.

In 2013, smarting from Romney's defeat at the hands of Obama in the 2012 election, Republican national committee chairman Reince Priebus commissioned an audit of the Republican defeat to identify why it had happened, and suggest ways the party could grow and win in the future.

The Republican strategists aimed their report squarely at making inroads among Hispanic voters. They flat out said that the party's standing with Latinos had gotten so dangerously low that if it didn't change, "our Party's appeal was in danger of shrinking to its core constituencies only."[1]

Having identified the problem dramatically, they proclaimed what they said was the solution, the only solution: they

demanded that Republicans embrace and champion compre-
hensive immigration reform.[2]

The pre-Trump Republicans of 2013 put it this way: "The
Republican Party needs to stop talking to itself. To stop talking
only to like-minded people, driving around in circles in an ideo-
logical cul-de-sac."[3]

In other words, we can win if we sellout and change our positions and rhetoric to suit the media.

Well, we didn't. The Republicans drew the line at another
round of amnesty for illegal immigrants, saying it would only
lead to more coming over the border.

Instead, the Republicans nominated Donald Trump, a president who attacked illegal immigrants, noting that among their
numbers were "rapists and murderers."[4]

The Democrats had a field day publicizing the remark and
claiming that it was Trump's death knell in his pursuit of the
Latino vote. He was accused of out-and-out racism and bias
against Hispanics.

Then Trump did himself one better and made his demand
for a Southern border wall to keep out illegal immigrants the
centerpiece of his campaign.

After Trump won, he battled hard to build his wall, grabbing
funds from every budget he could get his hands on to pay for it.

Democrats licked their chops. They figured they had drawn
a line in the sand, and that Trump had stepped over it. Now
he could not win the Hispanic vote, and would probably be
defeated for re-election.

But fortunately, the Democrats were dead wrong. The
2020 election shows clearly that the Hispanic/Latino vote is

trending Republican, impelled by Trump's policies and priorities. Regardless of who you think really won the 2020 election, everybody now agrees that the Hispanic vote, for the first time in history, swung dramatically to the Republicans. Trump's vote share among Hispanics grew by eight points between his 2016 victory against Hillary, and his 2020 run against Biden. Not only did Trump not repel Latino voters, he proved to be a positive magnet in attracting them!

Trump was supposed to lose Texas and Florida because he had alienated Hispanics. Yeah? He carried Texas by six points, and Florida by three.

MSN reported that on election night, 2020, Miami-Dade County gave the Democratic Party a panic attack. Florida was the first major swing state to report its ballots, and returns from overwhelmingly Hispanic—and heretofore, overwhelmingly Democratic—precincts showing the incumbent president making massive gains with a demographic they said he'd spent five years disparaging.

And in South Texas, in the famed Rio Grande Valley, it was the same story. Trump beat Biden.

In Zapata County, which *Time Magazine* describes as a patchwork of cattle ranches covered in prickly pear cactus that is 95 percent Hispanic, and that Hillary carried by thirty-three points, Trump won by five. The first Republican presidential win there since 1920.

And the tide rolled on! Hispanic and Latino counties in Texas—La Salle, Jim Wells, Kennedy, and Kleberg—flipped from Clinton to Trump. Laredo had the largest swing toward Trump of any big metro area.

Even in totally Democratic Hispanic regions like the South Bronx, Trump got five and six times more votes in 2020 than he did in 2016.

Overall, Trump's gains among Hispanics defied all the predictions. Democrats were stunned. How the hell did that happen, they wondered. We had a Republican president who opposed immigration reform and even built a wall to keep illegals out. And then he goes and gets 40 percent more Hispanic votes than Hillary got. What's going on?

I'll tell you my theory: Hispanics are patriots. They, their parents, and their ancestors voted with their feet to come to America. Behind them, they left governments dominated by socialism, corruption, drugs, and violence. When they saw the radical Left tearing America down, attacking the police, defacing our history, and displaying the same kind of corruption that ruined their own native countries, they were appalled.

In the Trump campaign, we figured there would be a big backlash among white high-school voters against the tactics of Antifa and the radical Left. There was, and we did gain, but less than we thought we would. Our big wins came among people who had *chosen* to be Americans. Not just those who were born here, but those who have wanted, all their lives, to be Americans, and were proud that they had made it.

The Hispanic vote for Trump rose 8 percent, and his Asian support went up 6 percent. These were the folks who are really determined to save America, the country they dreamed of.

Two-thirds of the Hispanic vote is cast in only seven states—Arizona, California, Florida, Nevada, Texas, Colorado, and New Mexico. While the African-American vote is more diffused around the country, the Latino vote is concentrated in a few swing states.

Trump and the Republicans did best among Hispanics in the Southeastern states, winning 47 percent in Florida, and 41 percent in Texas. In those states, Latino culture is more often integrated with that of their Anglo neighbors. The menu of any good restaurant in South Florida or Texas is full of Mexican dishes, for example.

There is less merging of the Hispanic and Anglo cultures in the Western states. In California, for example, the political hostility of the Anglo population against Mexican immigrants soils the state's history. Republican efforts—blocked by the federal courts—to require only English in schools, and to deprive illegal immigrant children of a free public education, have rankled the Latino population, leaving a sour taste in their mouths. As a result, only 21 percent of California's Latinos, and 31 percent of Arizona's, voted Republican.

Of course, the Hispanic vote is not monolithic. Because more than a dozen Spanish-speaking countries contribute immigrants to the United States—each of whose people have a different experience in their former lands—their opinions of Democrats, socialists, and Leftists vary considerably.

Cubans, Venezuelans, Colombians, and most Central Americans—with the experience of communism right before them all of their lives—voted heavily for Trump. The high proportion of the Hispanic population of Florida that comes from the Caribbean area, where communism is a real threat, propelled Trump to carry the state.

But the message that America's Latinos of all stripes sent to the Left is abundantly clear: This country is the best in the world, and we will not vote for any party that would deliver it into the hands of the socialists or communists.

A poll by the National Republican Senatorial Committee, taken in spring 2021, found how much Latinos disapprove of the left-wing agenda being pushed by the Democrats.

In the GOP poll:

- 58 percent of Latino voters said too many people in America are happy not to work and "just live off government assistance."
- 80 percent agreed that "public schools are failing."
- 67 percent felt that too many Americans "are losing our traditional values centered on faith, family, and freedom."
- 57 percent "opposed Democrat efforts to pack the Supreme Court with liberal justices."
- 72 percent agreed that "we should do what is necessary to control our Southern border."
- 65 percent opposed the Democrats' bill that would make it "illegal to ask voters for photo identification."
- 50 percent agreed that "many of the policies that Democrats say they want to help Latinos would really hurt Hispanic families."[5]

The End of Deportations

Not only does Biden make it much easier to sneak into the country, he makes it almost impossible to be kicked out.

No matter how serious the crime, the Biden policies are increasingly making it impossible to deport criminals, even if they are here illegally. Before Biden, any illegal immigrant who committed a violent crime would be subject to deportation.

But now they are welcome to stay.

Biden has issued an executive order stopping ICE from deporting illegal immigrants now in the United States, including thousands of murderers and rapists. Once these criminals had been arrested, convicted, and sentenced, and had served their time, they used to be turned over to ICE to be deported, because we didn't want them in our country anymore.

So in 2018, the United States, under the Trump administration, deported over seven hundred convicted murderers and four hundred rapists. But as radicals began to take over states and cities, they began to declare sanctuary cities and states. That means that when the murderers and rapists finally get out of jail, ICE can't deport them. They are here to stay. Practically none of those deported in 2018 would be deported under Biden's new orders.

They'd all be able to live right here in our neighborhoods, preying on our families.

Under the Biden order, the only people ICE can take into custody are those who are—at that very moment—already in prison, *and* in a jurisdiction where state and local laws permit the prison authorities to cooperate with ICE. The way it works is that in a state like Texas, for example, they will be turned over to ICE once their prison sentence is served. But in California and other sanctuary states, they won't be. They'll be released. These people are here illegally, have been convicted of aggravated felonies, and are now to be released onto the street.

And once they are out on the street, even if they just got out yesterday, they can stay in the United States forever, with Biden's blessing.

Biden also says that nobody can be deported for murders they committed ten or more years ago. But no state has a statute of limitations for murder. No matter how long ago the killing was, it can always be prosecuted. But the Biden order creates a statute of limitations for murder, banning deportations after ten years.

Dodge the law for a decade, and you're free to live here, regardless of what you did.

The new order also specifically provides that nobody can be deported for drug trafficking, no matter how much they sold. Twenty-two hundred drug traffickers were deported in 2018. Good riddance! But under Biden's new rules, they can't be sent back to their countries anymore. They're here to stay, selling drugs to our kids.

The Center for Immigration Studies examined all 95,000 illegal immigrants the United States deported in 2018 to see how their cases would have been handled under Biden's order. It found that only 4 percent would have been made to leave us. The rest could have stayed right here.

So of the 95,000 criminals deported in 2018, 91,000 would not have been deported under Biden's order. Only about 4,000 would now be thrown out.

The Biden order specifies that nobody can be deported for any of these crimes: drug crimes, simple assault, DUI, money laundering, property crimes, fraud, tax crimes, solicitation, or charges without convictions.

What about people who enter the country illegally, get arrested, get deported, and then turn around and come back here, again and again? No more deportations, says Biden's order.

One big problem is that, in sanctuary states like California, local law enforcement won't tell ICE whom they are releasing the next day. You'd think they'd call ICE and say, "We have a murderer and two rapists, all here illegally, getting out tomorrow at two o'clock. If you want to deport them, come by, and we'll turn them over to you." In Texas, they'll make that call. But in California, they won't. In fact, it's illegal under California law to notify ICE. So ICE has no idea who is getting out, when. Now, under Biden's new rules, ICE will never be notified, whatever the state wants, and the criminals will never be deported.

Rather than deport these folks who have committed violent crimes, Biden would give them food stamps, stimulus checks, and in-state college tuition. And Biden's secretary of health and human services, Xavier Becerra, wants to give them free health care, too.

Under Biden, once you make it over the border, you're probably never going to be deported. Once you're in, you're in. A powerful reason why hundreds of thousands risk coming.

The new Biden policy actually states that "If there is any question as to whether an individual falls into the category of posing a public safety threat, managers should err on the side of caution and postpone the individual's removal until a full assessment, in coordination with local Office of Chief Counsel, is conducted."[6] He or she gets the benefit of the doubt, and we have to spend even more tax dollars investigating whether he or she is a danger to us.

Oh, and one more thing: Biden says we can't call them "illegal immigrants," or worse, "illegal aliens." That would hurt their feelings. We have to say that they are just "undocumented," like they left their wallet at home that morning.

Now don't get me wrong, we are all descendants of immigrants. But there is a world of difference between those who obeyed our laws, waited their turn, and came here legally, and those who snuck in. The crime rate for legal immigrants is lower than for the population as a whole. They want to be good citizens, and the vast majority are.

17

Decriminalize
Crime

THE DEMOCRATIC LEFTIST ATTITUDE toward crime and law
and order differs sharply from that of the rest of the country.
Today's Left is truly radical and revolutionary.

Their language is upside down, right out of George Orwell's
book *1984*.

For example, Leftists say that looting is a fully legitimate form
of social protest. Vicky Osterweil, writing in *The New Inquiry*,
claims that "for most of America's history, one of the most righteous anti-white supremacist tactics available was looting."[1]
Looting, righteous? Go figure.

The preponderance of Black inmates in prisons is said by the
Left to be not so much due to that their committing the bulk of

the crimes, but because of the establishment's policy—or even its goal—of mass incarceration of Blacks and people of color.

The war on drugs is less a crusade to protect our children from addictive drugs, than a pretext to lock up Black people.

The Left says that the presumption of innocence, built into our judicial values, should allow criminals to be released right after their arrest, often without cash bail, even if it lets them back out on the streets within hours and nobody need worry about coming back to court.

The Left says that those who break our immigration laws and enter our country illegally are not criminals so much as heroes and pioneers.

The Left wants to cut the number of uniformed police and replace them with social workers and psychologists to stem violence and escalation. So the next time you worry that a criminal is trying to break into your home, call 911 and wait for a social worker to arrive.

The Left calls police shootings genocide of African Americans. Even though about half of the civilians killed by uniformed police officers in 2020 were white, and only a quarter were Black.

One particular quirk of the Left is its attitude toward gun control. Leftists want to take away guns from anyone who won't use them, but not from men on the street in high-crime neighborhoods at 4:00 a.m.

Back when New York City had upward of two thousand homicides a year, Mayors Giuliani and Bloomberg pushed stop-question-and-frisk legislation. If you were caught with an unlicensed loaded gun on the streets of New York, you would have faced a mandatory jail sentence of three years. Football stars, along with many others, were locked up under this law. No exceptions.

Cops began to see fewer thugs with guns on the street, and gun crimes plummeted. Stop-question-and-frisk turned out to be the most effective anti-crime law on the books.

But the Left decried it because Blacks were disproportionately arrested. Of course, it was because they had the guns and committed half of the murders (despite being only 12 percent of the population). So the liberal lawyers talked the liberal judges into throwing out the law.

What a blow for justice! Homicides—primarily among minorities—soared.

Meanwhile, the Left endorses its own version of stop-and-frisk, going into middle-class communities and knocking on doors of hunters who would use their firearms on deer, while letting those who have human targets go free and unmolested.

Indeed, the progressive Left has a totally different idea of crime than the rest of the country. To the rest of us, the criminal is to blame. To the Left, society and racism are responsible. Jail is not primarily a way to deter crimes or to punish those who commit them. Rather, Leftists see it as a form of racial apartheid, reminiscent of South Africa. The real injustice, they say, is condemning the criminal to prison. The fault, they believe, lies not with those who commit the crimes, but with the process— the police, prosecutors, defense attorneys, juries, and judges that catch, prosecute, and convict the criminals. The real crimes here, they believe, are not murder or rape or robbery, but rather, racism, discrimination, and poverty.

One suspects that the Left sees crime rather like Robin Hood did in medieval England—as an opportunity to take from the rich and give to the poor. Rather than leave this particular task to the experts at the IRS, they seem to root for the robbers and against the cops.

The Left's goal is not to reduce crime by cutting the number of murders, rapes, and robberies. It is to reduce punishment, incarceration, and harsh sentencing by decriminalizing crime. The decriminalization of pot is an obvious example of a successful policy. But by meting out short sentences and allowing defendants to avoid showing up for trial without sanctions, the Left is moving quickly to eliminate the consequences of all criminal behavior—the decriminalization of crime! Crime and punishment are being replaced by crime and looking the other way.

The victim? He or she is just part of the vast racist conspiracy, and therefore deserves what he or she gets. Collateral damage. Hey, what goes around, comes around. How inconvenient for the Left when the culprit and the victim are both people of color!

Eighty-nine percent of all murders of Black people in the United States are committed by Black people, and 79 percent of the killings of whites are by whites. So how do these stats indicate that the criminal justice system is racist?

Because of these left-wing attitudes, all but endorsing crime, it is sprouting like grass growing through the cracks in the sidewalks of America's neglected cities, carefully cultivated from the seeds of resentment, envy, and social jealousy sown by ambitious Democratic gardeners.

That crime was down under Trump, and is up under Biden, is a simple fact that most voters—including even Democrats—acknowledge. What is more complicated is how crime has soared inside less than a year into the Biden presidency.

Once again, the advice of former Chicago mayor Rahm Emanuel—that "no good crisis go to waste"—is responsible.

In 2020, the despicable murder of George Floyd at the hands of Minneapolis police provided the crisis, the spark, that inflamed the Black community and ignited the Black Lives Matter (BLM) movement.

Choosing Pro-Crime Prosecutors

Floyd's murder, and the backlash of justifiable outrage it spawned, has led to the election of radicals as district attorneys around the country in key high-crime cities in the municipal elections.

People only notice bad weather when it's raining. When crime is low, it becomes a non-issue. Instead of writing about murders and dead bodies, the media focuses on police misconduct. Successful crime-fighting mayors like New York City's Rudy Giuliani have found that their biggest enemy is their own success. As they reduce the crime rate, they erode the issue that underscored their popularity and political viability.

Amid this attitude of complacency about crime, it was comparatively easy for billionaire George Soros to pour millions into the candidacies of ultra-Left radicals and get them elected district attorney.

The arsonists now run the fire departments.

Since our justice system is adversarial, electing prosecutors who are, at best, soft on crime—and in some cases, pro-crime—means that the judicial pendulum will veer toward letting criminals go free, and citizens unprotected. It's like assigning the fox to prosecute chicken killers.

And some of these leftist prosecutors are a piece of work.

George Soros pumped $2.5 million into the PAC funding for the campaign of George Gascón for DA of Los Angeles County.

LA is plagued by street gangs. So they passed a law to fight them that lets judges add years to their sentence if the criminal is part of a gang. But to invoke the law, the district attorney has to ask for the enhanced sentence. DA Gascón won't do it. And without the DA moving for an enhancement, it can't happen.

In early 2021, in Los Angeles, a member of the infamous MS-13 gang beat up a woman so badly that she had to be hospitalized. The deputy DA—under Gascón—said, "It was clearly a gang case. The gang allegation should have been filed." But Gascón didn't let him do it. So the assailant will get off with a light sentence.

Gascón is not only refusing to ask for harsher sentences on gang members, he is now dismantling the Hardcore Gang Unit of his office that works in collaboration with local law enforcement.

California also has a "three-strikes" law, where if you are convicted of three violent felonies, you can get a life sentence with no parole. But Gascón won't enforce that law either. To get a "strike" on your record, the DA has to ask the judge to do it. But Gascón won't even ask, so repeat criminals never get to three strikes.

One more example: The law in California says that if you kill someone, and there are special circumstances, you have to get the death penalty or life without parole. For example, if you kill during a rape, or ambush your victim, or commit an especially brutal killing, the DA can request a sentence of death or of life without parole. But the DA has to ask for it and give the facts to the judge. Gascón won't do that either.

The assistant DAs in Gascón's own office are so fed up with his policies that they are even risking their jobs by suing their boss to make him enforce the various statutes he's ignoring.

On the East Coast, another George Soros gift to America is Larry Krasner, the Philadelphia County DA who got $1.5 million from Soros for his race.

Usually, candidates for DA vie with each other to show how tough they are on crime. But in the Orwellian world of the far-Left, Krasner ran on how often he cut back charges or dropped cases against violent offenders.

Five months after he was elected, he demonstrated his pro-crime bias by cutting a deal with defense attorneys for two career criminals who killed a Philadelphia police officer, allowing their clients to escape the death penalty. These attorneys only got their sweetheart deal after coincidentally donating over $4,000 to Krasner's campaign.

In another case, the *Washington Free Beacon* reported that "Krasner reached another controversial plea deal with a career criminal who shot a Philadelphia deli owner with an AK-47 during an armed robbery. Krasner's campaign contributor, Philip Steinberg, was the lawyer for the shooter and got him a sweet plea deal. Just three and a half years for aggravated assault."[2] It was aggravated, all right.

Under Krasner, crime in Philadelphia has gotten out of control. In 2019, 386 people were murdered. In 2020, it was up to 500, and 5 times that many were shot. City of Brotherly Love.

Chesa Boudin, another Soros darling whom the leftist billionaire got elected DA in San Francisco, has some background.

His parents are Kathy Boudin and David Gilbert, members of the Weather Underground. When Chesa was one year old, Mom was busted for murder in the Brinks robbery of 1981, and got twenty years. Dad got seventy-five years for killing two cops and a security guard. Then Chesa was adopted by wolves—Bill

Ayers—remember, Obama's mentor—and Bernadine Dohrn, both Weather Underground members. And now he's DA of San Francisco. How crazy are these people?

George Soros, the man who puts up the money behind this dangerous attempt to put criminals ahead of victims in our largest cities, doesn't have to worry about street gangs. He's reportedly worth upward of $8 billion and lives on an estate in Bedford Hills, in New York's Westchester County.[3]

Now the crazy Left is pressing Biden to appoint radicals like Krasner, Gascón, and Boudin as US attorneys around the country—a dangerous move.

The Hill reports that, "in March 2021, a coalition of advocacy groups sent a letter to Biden calling on him to nominate federal prosecutors 'capable of delivering fair sentencing, rearranging prosecutorial priorities and rooting out misconduct.'"[4] In other words, letting criminals go free.

In federal court, US attorneys rule. Their power to bring indictments and to plea-bargain charges is enormous. So when Biden is announcing that he will appoint the US attorneys similar to the radical district attorneys Soros and his crew have elected, it means gigantic changes in the policies of federal court.

In the past thirty years, there has been a move to try criminal gangs, particularly drug dealers, in federal, as opposed to state, courts. In fact, state prosecutors will often work with US attorneys to transfer drug cases to federal court, because the sentences are so much longer there, and the opportunities for leniency through plea-bargaining so much more limited.

But now, Biden is threatening to reverse the tables and make federal criminal justice as porous as the state process by naming left-wing radicals as US attorneys.

Rachel Barkow, a leftist professor at the New York University School of Law, says that because of the power that prosecutors wield, Biden's appointments could make or break his "reform" agenda.[5]

She argues that "it wouldn't be enough to just focus on the courts as the place where you're committed to diversifying and getting a reform-minded perspective in there [aka a left-wing agenda]. You absolutely have to have the same attitude when it comes to the U.S. attorney's posts."[6]

Victimizing the Police

During the election campaign of 2020, leftist demonstrators called for defunding of police forces throughout the country. Biden fueled the Left's momentum by calling for the diversion of funds intended for the police to go, instead, to social workers, family counselors, and psychologists.

New York City slashed $1 billion of police funding, and other cities followed suit. The results were catastrophic. In the first few months of 2021, murders in America's twenty largest cities rose by 25 percent. But in the nine cities where police funds were cut or diverted, they soared by even more—68 percent.

Understandably, police officers responded to public hostility by hanging up their badges and leaving the force. Retirements from the New York City Police Department rose by 75 percent.

And those who have stayed on are hobbled by new laws and regulations.

In New York City, echoing the Biden policy on the Southern border, those who have been arrested have been soon released, only to commit violent crimes again. Cash bail has been abolished. Those who once would have been incarcerated are now released on their own recognizance, rarely to be seen in court again.

Until, that is, they strike again.

A twenty-two-year-old New Yorker was arrested after robbing four businesses. After he was busted, he was quickly freed, only to burglarize yet another store in twenty-four hours. He then went on a spree and broke into five more businesses over four days.

Fueling voluntary retirements, cops don't see the point in risking their lives to apprehend criminals, only to meet them on the same street corners days later.

And the Left isn't finished yet.

Democrats in the New York State Legislature are pushing a "clean slate" bill that would automatically wipe away criminal records for a vast range of serious crimes, including violent offenses. As reported in the *New York Post,* State Senate Republican Minority Leader Robert Ortt warns: "If enacted, a bank owner wouldn't know if he is hiring a convicted embezzler, and a single mother wouldn't know if she is moving across the hall from a convicted killer."[7]

The radicals who control America's legislative chambers are seeking further to hobble police through a new Police Accountability Act. Introduced in New York State by Attorney General Letitia James, it would raise the threshold for the justified use of force. Now cops can use force due to "necessity." The bill would raise the standard to one of "absolute last resort," mandating that police officers only use force "after all other alternatives have been exhausted."[8]

The most pernicious of the proposed "reforms" that radicals are pushing would end the current law granting police officers conditional immunity from civil liability for misconduct or excessive use of force. Under current law, someone whose rights may have been violated can sue the city or the police department, but not the police officer individually for damages.

Justified or not, complaints about excessive force are widespread. *USA Today* reports that 23,000 police have been investigated for use of excessive force over the past decade.[9] Currently, police officers are immune from civil lawsuits for the use of excessive force, violating the constitutional rights of citizens. But the Left has been pressing for lifting that immunity.

Without this immunity, every time a cop arrests someone, or uses force to restrain rioters or to catch escaping suspects, he or she would be subject to a potential lawsuit. Ending this immunity would make the police force nothing more than a group of expensive, decorative, unformed officers who dare not do anything to protect the public.

Consider the risks of being a conscientious police officer in this new climate where cops are reviled, spat upon, insulted, and degraded by the citizenry they are sworn to protect.

Police officers and their families must consider the risks to their lives. Last year, as many cops were shot and killed in the line of duty (89) as killed a civilian (81). And the majority of those whom police killed were not Black.

If cops were liable to be sued for civil damages for use of force, routine complaints from civilians could lead to an officer being buried in legal fees or fined so much that he would lose his house, his job, his health care, and his pension. With police salaries in the NYPD starting at $42,000, and rising to only $85,000 after five years, a cop probably does not have sufficient assets to take such liability in stride. One false step as the officer tries to protect a citizen could ruin the work of a lifetime in earning a living for his or her family and children.

And the stress of the job all too often is not offset by what good the officer can accomplish. When an officer has to risk death, their house, and their career to act to apprehend a suspect or prevent a crime, he or she may understandably hesitate.

And many just leave the force.

Let's pause for a moment to consider what the motivation of the Left is for pushing for individual civil liability for cops. It's not to get money for the victim. He can already sue the city and the police department, both of whom have deep pockets. But the average police officer has no real assets. Not much money there. The goal in making cops individually liable cannot be financial. It is social. The Left seeks to hold the club of liability over the heads of the police to dissuade them from doing their job of protecting the public.

Using the Crime Issue to Win

The surge in crime that accompanied the advent of the Biden administration is having a devastating impact on the president's ratings.

A poll by *The Washington Post* and ABC News found that only 38 percent approved of Biden's efforts to reduce crime, while 48 percent disapproved. The poll found that more Americans believe crime is an "extremely serious" or "very serious" problem in the area where they live, than have felt that way in any poll in the past twenty years.[10]

And in the nation as a whole, 59 percent of adults believe crime is extremely or very serious in the United States as a whole—the highest figure in three years.

House Democratic Whip James Clyburn (D-SC) said it best

when he compared the "Defund the police" slogan with rioters chanting, "Burn, baby, burn!" in the 1960s. Clyburn said, "I think [the demand for defunding police] is cutting the throats of the party. I know exactly where my constituents are. They are against that, and I'm against that."[11]

Clyburn is right. The Left's animosity toward police will cost the Democrats legions of voters who are moderates ideologically, but in the midst of a national crime wave, do not agree that we should defund the police.

The crime issue is particularly toxic for the Democrats, because it is obvious to voters that it was not nearly as bad a problem before Biden was elected. Back in 2019, and before, crime had fallen out of the headlines and faded in popular consciousness. But after Biden's election, the movement to defund the police, and the vilification of dedicated, responsible, fair, and hardworking police officers has set the crime rate soaring. So who is to blame? Figure it out!

18

Dumbing Down Education

L IKE A STREET-CORNER DRUG dealer, Democrats peddle dreams to their voters—fantasies, illusions, and wishful thinking.

Two delusions, in particular, predominate in the propaganda of the Democrats. First, the imaginary increase in income the Left claims it's promoting, and second, that public schools are giving their children a good education. Neither illusion is based in reality. While paychecks are growing, their value is shrinking as prices outpace our earnings. And our children may get glowing report cards to bring home, but they're only the result of dumbing down standards and asking less and less from students.

Spurred by the teacher's union, the Left brags about improvement in schools.

These two illusions—that your children are getting a good education, and that your income is rising—let the Democrats win elections.

But then, Bush 43 challenged the education delusion when Congress passed his bill to require standardized testing of fourth- and eighth-grade students, and of their teachers. Before these testing requirements, the only measure a concerned parent had of his or her child's progress was a report card, usually filled out by a teacher who was trying to look good.

At first, teachers and administrators improved their performance, and both reading and math scores rose now that they were being tested. But in the past decade, they have dropped back again. Trump's secretary of education, Betsy DeVos, said that "Two out of three of our nation's children aren't proficient readers, and the gap between the highest and lowest performing students is widening."[1]

Thirty percent of prospective recruits fail the Armed Forces Qualification Tests. The main culprit is our schools.

Under Bush's No Child Left Behind Act, the lower test scores automatically triggered a major increase in federal aid to underperforming schools. But it didn't work. Despite the extra dollars, test scores continued to drop.

So the Left had a simple answer: lower educational standards so more kids—particularly minority kids—would pass.

My heart breaks when I pass a proud and buoyant group of largely minority students assembled—in their royal-blue graduation garb—in front of a New York City school. They are so thrilled to get their diplomas, and their parents are so proud. But little do they suspect that it is a fraud, a palliative, to succeed in such an environment.

They think their kids are high jumpers, clearing a bar high up in the air, but was easier to clear.

Never mind that they weren't getting an education in their schools, or that they weren't being equipped with basic workplace skills such as literacy and arithmetic. It felt good for parents to see their children in academic gowns on graduation day. That euphoria helped the liberal big-city schools perpetrate a myth—that all kids were getting a decent education.

When Republicans and conservatives began to push charter schools in earnest—citing proof that their test scores were higher than in regular public schools—the liberals and the Democrats tried to shut them down. New York State's legislature still will not permit more than one hundred charter schools in the entire state!

And when the Leftists who run New York's public schools find that minorities are not performing, they jigger the system, lower the standards, and put their thumbs on the scale to create the false impression of progress.

In the 1960s and 1970s, I worked with Congressman Herman Badillo, New York's first Puerto Rican member of Congress. Back then, he was a liberal Democrat who came very close to being the city's first—and, at the time this book goes to press, only—Hispanic mayor.

Later in his life, when he moved to the Right and became a Republican, he was appointed by Mayor Rudy Giuliani and New York's Governor George Pataki to be chancellor of the City University of New York (CUNY). He was appalled at the state to which this once proud and distinguished institution had sunk. Where once, it had graduated the likes of Henry Kissinger, Felix

Frankfurter, Bernard Baruch, Ed Koch, Badillo himself, and my father, its standards had crashed due to leftist pressure for open admissions—let everybody in. It had gotten so bad that a CUNY degree became worthless.

Then Badillo changed everything. Now, anyone can still get admitted after high school, but they have to pass a test showing that they can do college-level work. If they fail, they can remain at the university, taking remedial courses. But nobody matriculates into the college without passing the test. Soon, CUNY became one of the most prestigious universities in the country again and opened the door for tens of thousands of qualified minority students.

The Black Lives Matter movement has compounded the problem by pushing for higher, feel-good grades and lower standards.

The bugle call for retreat from higher school standards was sounded before the 2020 election, when Bernie Sanders and Joe Biden agreed on a "unity platform" that called for an "end to the use of high-stakes tests." Instead, they said, grading student performance should rely on "evidence-based approaches to student assessment that rely on multiple and holistic measures that better represent student achievement."[2] In other words, no testing. Rely on what the teachers say is going on. Take their word for it.

The Left also complains that testing can "lead to discrimination against students, particularly those with disabilities, students of color, low-income students, and English language learners."[3] In other words, we don't want to know the truth about how our kids are doing. Just send us good news, even if it's more fantasy than reality.

Instead of rigorous standardized tests, the Left deludes parents, particularly in minority families, by sending home feel-good report cards, boasting of non-existent student progress, and assuring that all is well.

Disregarding the real best interests of students of color, the Left is so dumbing down the quality of the education that schools offer diplomas that mean little or nothing.

That these urban schools are bad is nothing new. But that the Left and their Democratic puppets are deliberately seeking to lower their standards is both new and tragic.

Oregon, for example, has suspended a requirement for a basic-skills test in math, reading, and writing to graduate from high school. The AP reports that the new law "is being praised by advocates as a way to rethink education standards."[4]

The Left hates it when a student in a public school gets into special classes for gifted kids. They say that these classes promote segregation. Even though the standards to attend these classes are colorblind, they say the concept of student giftedness has led to considerable inequities.

California's and New York City's public school systems recently ended advanced math classes, saying that they were disproportionately white. It makes no difference if the disproportionate number of white students reflects objective measurements like test scores, the Black Lives Matter folks denounce it like it was the old segregated Southern schools.

I was in special classes for my entire twelve years of public schooling. Best of all, I attended Stuyvesant High School, arguably the best in the country. But you had to pass an admissions exam to get in. Still do.

But Mayor Bill de Blasio was trying to dilute the quality of New York's special schools by admitting minority students who fail the admissions test. Fortunately, the incoming mayor, Eric

Adams, seems to be committed to test-based admissions to special schools.

Indeed, the goal of the Left has shifted from promoting equal opportunity to seeking equal outcomes. This trend has led to grade inflation and a general decline in standards. Everybody gets an A.

The Vancouver school system has eliminated honors courses as part of a push to foster inclusivity and equity in the classroom. The board had previously eliminated the high-school honors English program, and honors math and science will now get the axe as well. "By phasing out these courses, all students will have access to an inclusive model of education, and all students will be able to participate in the curriculum fulsomely,"[5] the school board claimed.

So what if bright kids, of any race, have to sit in class, bored out of their gourds while the others catch up? But it is these successful students who hold the key to America's future. Don't dumb them down. Challenge the others to brighten up.

Former Louisiana State Senator Conrad Appel, an education reformer, describes the dumbing down of schools as "woke equity at its worst. Deprive students, both majority and minority, of rigor in order to artificially equalize results for all. Destroy the quality of the education of all students by absolving them of high expectations and mandatory commitment. Degrade minorities by promoting the notion that math must be dumbed down so that they can succeed as well as everyone else. These attitudes will carry young people far in life, NOT!"[6]

Parents Revolt Against Woke Schools

Increasingly, parents are actively getting involved in checking the move to diminish standards in public schools and to use them as vehicles for indoctrinating—and inoculating—students.

Echoing the grass roots Tea Party Movement of ten years ago, America's public school parents are speaking out against school boards that promote teaching about Critical Race Theory and sexual diversity. Demonstrators are speaking out at board meetings and demanding that the standards they promote parallel mainstream American values and not the twisted views of the radical Left. They also object to a government requirement that their children be vaccinated against COVID, even if their parents object.

The number of new COVID cases has plummeted due to widespread vaccinations, now that over 70 percent of the country is fully vaccinated. Why, the parents say, should everyone, even little children, be forced to get the shot if their parents do not approve? If those who have gotten the shots are immune, they ask, what danger do the unvaccinated pose to them? So isn't it their own business—not the government's—whether they are vaccinated or not?

The Left resents and fears the incursion of angered parents into the swindle their kids are getting in school. Defeated Democratic candidate for Virginia Governor, Terry McAuliffe, stumbled badly—and lost the election in part because of it—when he applauded his decision, in his first term, to veto legislation that required schools to alert parents when there was sexually explicit content in school instructional materials. "I'm not going to let parents come into schools and actually take books out and make their own decision," he said. He further cooked his candidacy when he added, "I don't think parents should be telling schools what they should teach."[7]

Biden's attorney general, Merrick B. Garland, ran afoul of the burgeoning movement of aggrieved parents when, responding to a complaint from the National Association of School Boards (NASB), he asked the FBI to investigate whether parents who loudly object at school board meetings are, in fact, domestic terrorists.

Asra Nomani, the vice president of investigations and strategy at Parents Defending Education, showed photos of parents and asked, "This is what a domestic terrorist looks like?" She said Biden was "criminalizing parenting," and said "you owe the people of America a swift apology."[8]

House Minority Leader Kevin McCarthy (R-Cal) says Biden is "weaponizing" the Justice Department to "target parents seeking to be involved in their children's education." He added, "Parents have a fundamental right to be lawfully involved in their children's education. We should encourage family participation in our school systems, not baselessly attack opposing views because some liberal education officials and special interest groups see it as a threat to the power they want to have over what children learn in America's classrooms."[9]

Recently, a Minnesota school board demonstrated the lengths to which education professionals will go to promote their values in schools. There, the board is making straight students pretend they are in a gay or lesbian relationship.

When I was in school, we presented Romeo and Juliet in school plays, but now Minnesota features Morgan and Terence. "Morgan" is a boy who is "very active" in his school's LGBTQ club, while "Terence" is a student who wants to have sex with

"Morgan," and is not publicly out as gay. The plot thickens: Morgan outlines a plan for the two students to secretly meet, according to the curriculum, and "make a decision about whether to have sex."[10]

The more the Democrats, and their teachers' union allies, promote these kinds of nutty positions on education, the more inroads we can make among suburban, college-educated parents who form the core of the white Democratic base.

A Final Thought: Pro-Life *and* Pro-Choice

The gender gap—the tendency of women to vote for Democrats, even as men back Republicans—has been a defining reality in elections ever since the early 1970s. It has always stemmed from Democratic support for reproductive choice, and Republican backing of pro-life policies.

Supreme Court watchers are expecting a definitive ruling on abortion before the election of 2022. If the Court, despite its conservative majority, leaves *Roe v. Wade* as the law of the land, permitting abortion, the fears of pro-choice women may abate sufficiently to lead them to explore other issues that might make them more interested in the Republican agenda.

But recent advances in medicine and technology have made it increasingly possible for the fetus to live outside the womb at an earlier age. The standard for viability set by the Court in *Roe v Wade* was the start of the third trimester (twenty-six weeks). But now, a fetus can live outside the womb as early as twenty-three or twenty-four weeks, and scientists are working on preserving them from twenty-one weeks on.

Doesn't this raise the possibility of a third way? Not either abortion or requiring the mother to give birth, but rather, early birth where the fetus would be surgically removed from the womb and kept viable in artificial wombs or incubators?

We can separate the goals of the pro-choice and pro-life movements, and achieve them both: termination of an unwanted pregnancy, and preservation of the life of a fetus!

Such a plan should include enhanced subsidies of adoption so the fetus could find a loving home after birth, and financial compensation and incentives to the pregnant woman for avoiding abortion.

With 700,000 abortions in the United States last year, but only 135,000 adoptions, let's change the odds and defuse this red-hot issue in our politics.

Conclusion

WE CANNOT READ THE plans of the woke Left without understanding, in a way that we never have, the true stakes involved in the elections of 2022 and 2024.

Are the gains of generations of American families to be burned alive on the coals of woke envy? Is all that we have achieved as a nation, and as families, to be held hostage in order to punish us for slaves we never owned (and our ancestors died to free), discrimination we never practiced, and racism we never felt in our hearts?

Are our children to be taught to hate and envy one another? Is the emerging post-racial era in our society to be forfeit in the new cancel culture? Are our heroes to be debased, and our great past presidents to be demeaned as slave-owning imperialists?

Is brotherhood to be sacrificed for hatred? Is reconciliation to be wiped out in the name of meting out what the Left calls "equity"—balancing the accounts of history by robbing the present to pay the supposed debts of the past?

Are the shared sacrifices of the past—what Lincoln, in his first inaugural address, called the "mystic chords of memory and the better angels of our nature"[1]—to be swept aside with each swipe of the woke guillotine of the cancel culture?

Is our blessed democracy to be debased by altered ballots, phony signatures, and ghost voters, all because the burden of voter identification is too onerous?

And consider whether the hard-won gains of women who have liberated themselves from the velvet slavery of enforced domesticity, are to be compromised once again by the avarice of men, now cross-dressed, and perhaps surgically altered, to masquerade as women.

Are the rungs of the ladder we all need to use to climb above our current stations in life to be sawed away by what President Bush 43 called "the soft bigotry of low expectations"?[2]

Are we to be yoked to a technocracy where our innermost thoughts can be read by Chinese and American Big Tech masters?

Are we to be drowned in a sea of illegal immigration?

Will crime again rule our streets at night?

Will blind partisanship, motivated by class hatred and envy, so divide us that we become one another's enemies? Or will we again follow the advice of Abraham Lincoln, that "we are not enemies, but friends. We must not be enemies. Though passion may have strained, it must not break our bonds of affection."[3]

Acknowledgments

I N THIS BOOK AND in my media commentary, I am very indebted to several people who send me material, often unsolicited and uncompensated. I fine their help very valuable. My esteemed sources often include: Bruce Nevins, Stephen Moore (of The Committee to Unleash Prosperity), James Edwards, Chuck Brooks, Steven Emerson, David Steinman, and John Jordan.

I am also deeply indebted to John and Jim McLaughlin for their polling data that is both accurate and insightful. (The best pollsters in politics. Perhaps the only good ones).

Among media outlets, there are two kinds of commentators in America: those who read *The Washington Times* and those who don't. Those who do, access reality. Those who don't dwell in an alternate reality to be jolted awake every election day.

Special thanks to my bosses and colleagues at NewsMax: Chris Ruddy, Elliot Jacobson, Christopher Wallace (not that one, the NM guy!), Rob Schmitt, Sean Spicer, Grant Stinchfield, Greg Kelly, Heather Childers, Dave Wasser, Gary Kanofsky, and John Bachman.

And thank you too to my friend who has helped me through such difficult recent times, Doug DePierro.

And to the foundation of my political insights, Eileen McGann.

Notes

Chapter 1

1. Hearing on Verification, Security, and Paper Records for Our Nation's Electronic Voting Systems: Hearing Before the Committee on House Administration, House of Representatives, One Hundred Ninth Congress, Second Session, Hearing Held in Washington, D.C., September 28, 2006; U.S. Government Printing Office, 2007.

Chapter 2

1. https://www.americanprogressaction.org/issues/democracy/reports/2020/08/06/178300/secretaries-state-crucial-protecting-african-american-voters/.
2. https://nypost.com/2021/10/13/mark-zuckerberg-spent-419m-on-nonprofits-ahead-of-2020-election-and-got-out-the-dem-vote/.
3. https://alumni.tip.duke.edu/team_member/jocelyn-benson/.
4. https://www.washingtonexaminer.com/news/judge-rules-michigan-sec-state-broke-law-absentee-ballot.
5. Ibid.
6. https://www.realclearpolitics.com/articles/2019/02/22/illegal_ballot_harvesting_a_looming_issue_in_arizona_.html#!.

7. https://www.motherjones.com/politics/2018/11/brian-kemps-win-in
-georgia-tainted-by-voter-suppression-stacey-abrams/.
8. https://www.usatoday.com/story/news/factcheck/2020/11/18/fact
-check-partly-false-claim-stacey-abrams-2018-race/6318836002/.
9. https://www.cnn.com/2021/05/26/politics/jody-hice-georgia-elections
-secretary-of-state-race/index.html.

Chapter 3
1. http://www.capoliticalreview.com/capoliticalnewsandviews/2020
-election-over-one-million-ineligible-persons-registered-to-vote-in
-california/.
2. https://www.sentencingproject.org/publications/locked-out-2020
-estimates-of-people-denied-voting-rights-due-to-a-felony-conviction/.

Chapter 4
1. https://www.christianitytoday.com/news/2008/april/obama-they-cling
-to-guns-or-religion.html.
2. Conversation with Jared Kushner on April 17, 2020.

Chapter 5
1. Conversation with Jared Kushner on April 17, 2020.
2. https://www.google.com/search?client=safari&rls=en&q=coronavirus
eaths+us&ie=UTF-8&oe=UTF-8.

Chapter 6
1. https://www.cbsnews.com/news/jeff-flake-full-transcript-speech
-senate-floor-trump-sustained-attack-on-press/.
2. https://www.azcentral.com/story/news/politics/arizona/2017/11/19/
jeff-flake-y-trump-twitter-attacks-arizona-senator-jeff-flake-calls
-flakes-political-career-toast/879416001/.
3. https://www.nbcnews.com/politics/politics-news/trump-sen-corker
-couldn-t-get-elected-dog-catcher-n813621.
4. Ibid.
5. https://www.ksn.com/news/national-world/trump-boasts-of-bigger
-nuclear-button-than-north-koreas/.
6. https://www.reuters.com/article/us-usa-trump-europe-idUSKBN18K34D.
7. https://www.nato.int/cps/en/natohq/news_171458.htm.
8. https://dailycaller.com/2021/06/29/cnn-loses-nearly-half-viewers-2020
-2021/.
9. https://gaffebateau.com/story/entertainment/tv/2021/06/30/fox-news.

Chapter 7
1. https://www.politico.com/news/2021/06/30/kamala-harris-office
-dissent-497290/.

2. Ibid.
3. Ibid.

Chapter 8

1. https://www.oleantimesherald.com/news/nation/poll-majority-of
-voters-blame-dem-policies-for-rising-inflation/article_8be2bdfb
-b880-501c-84e5-520afb72cee8.html.

Chapter 9

1. https://www.washingtonexaminer.com/news/rahm-emanuel-reprises
-never-let-a-crisis-go-to-waste-catchphrase-amid-coronavirus
-pandemic.
2. https://www.msn.com/en-us/news/politics/majority-of-republicans
-say-2020-election-was-invalid-poll/ar-BB1e1ggc.
3. Schenck v. United States, 249 U.S. 47 (1919).
4. Confessore, Nicholas. "Jeb Bush Draws on Family Dynasty for Fund-
Raising Efforts," *New York Times*, July 10, 2015.
5. http://www.touchngo.com/lglcntr/akstats/statutes/title15/
chapter15/section360.htm.
6. https://fivethirtyeight.blogs.nytimes.com/2012/12/27/as-swing
-districts-dwindle-can-a-divided-house-stand/.

Chapter 10

1. https://thehill.com/regulation/court-battles/553460-lawsuit-from
-stephen-miller-group-alleges-racial-discrimination-in.
2. Ibid.
3. https://www.cbsnews.com/news/yellen-harris-rapid-recovery-program
-watch-live-stream-today-2021-06-15/.
4. https://www.waterford.org/education/equity-vs-equality-in-education/.
5. https://compcenternetwork.org/news-events/events/6830/
us-department-education-equity-summit-series.
6. https://www.washingtontimes.com/news/2021/jun/11/james-lankford
-grills-xavier-becerra-birthing-peop/.
7. https://cnsnews.com/article/national/emma-riley/democrats-bar
-female-athletes-testifying-equality-act-hearing.
8. https://thespectator.info/2021/03/24/dem-lawmakers-sell-out-women
-ban-female-athletes-planning-to-testify-against-equality-act/.
9. https://www.amazon.com/Animal-Farm-George-Orwell/dp/
0451526341.
10. https://cnsnews.com/blog/craig-bannister/cnn-no-consensus-criteria
-assigning-sex-birth.
11. https://liberty4lifeorg.files.wordpress.com/2019/04/gender-dysphoria
-in-children-american-college-of-pediatricans-2018.pdf.

Chapter 11

1. Goldstein, Jacob, *Money: The True Story of a Made-Up Thing*, Hachette Books, New York, 2020.
2. Ibid., p.10.

Chapter 12

1. https://trendingpolitics.com/it-happened-here-are-eight-fake-news -narratives-about-trump-the-media-has-admitted-were-always- wrong/.
2. https://www.businessinsider.co.za/daily-mail-authenticated-hunter -biden-laptop-images-2021-4.
3. https://www.youtube.com/watch?v=fKK74bMmJa8.
4. https://hannity.com/media-room/breaking-national-intel-director- says-hunter-biden-emails-not-russian-disinformation-campaign/.
5. https://deadline.com/2021/01/simon-schuster-cancels-sen-josh -hawley-book-witnessing-disturbing-deadly-insurrection-capitol -1234666926/.
6. Ibid.
7. https://en.wikipedia.org/wiki/Common_carrier.

Chapter 13

1. https://americansforprosperity.org/the-house-passed-the-pro-act-what -does-that-mean-for-independent-contractors/.

Chapter 14

1. https://www.medgadget.com/2021/06/the-active-pharmaceutical -ingredient-market-to-stand-tall-based-on-technological-abetments .html.
2. https://www.urbandictionary.com/define.php?term=Useful%20Idiot.
3. https://asia.nikkei.com/Politics/International-relations/Biden-says -US-must-own-the-future-in-rivalry-with-China.
4. https://chinapower.csis.org/chinese-companies-global-500/.
5. https://chinaownsus.com/app/uploads/2021/03/ChinaOwnsUs_ WhitePaper_Mar2021.pdf.
6. https://www.axios.com/working-for-china-1515542281-d4bc0ab4 -bed6-4085-a26e-c5d7c66be74c.html.
7. https://www.foxnews.com/world/how-much-of-the-united-states -does-china-really-own.
8. https://www.axios.com/china-exploits-us-investment-to-conquer -media-1515429178-a5b1554c-acc8-4817-8cb8-218faae2d8b3.html.
9. https://abcnews.go.com/Business/wireStory/us-brings-charges -chinese-tech-giant-huawei-68967060.
10. https://www.wsj.com/articles/the-hunter-biden-laptop-is-real -11625868661.

11. https://www.worldtribune.com/its-that-bad-hunters-laptop-confirms
    -joe-was-direct-beneficiary-of-deals/.
12. Ibid.
13. https://www.wsj.com/articles/the-hunter-biden-laptop-is-real
    -11625868661.
14. https://www.newsmax.com/us/china-biden-bidencenter-upenn/2020/
    10/28/id/994198/.

Chapter 15
1. Friday, Nancy. *Jealousy*. William Morrow & Co; 1st edition (August 1,
   1985).

Chapter 16
1. https://talkingpointsmemo.com/dc/6-big-takeaways-from-the-rnc-s
   -incredible-2012-autopsy.
2. Ibid.
3. Ibid.
4. https://remezcla.com/culture/trump-referred-immigrants-rapists
   -murderers-again/.
5. https://duckduckgo.com/?q=%E2%80%9Care+losing+our+traditional
   +values+centered+on+faith%2C+family+and+freedom.%E2
   %80%9D&t=osx&ia=web.
6. www.azag.gov/sites/default/files/2021-04/AR_AZ_00004699.pdf.

Chapter 17
1. https://thenewinquiry.com/in-defense-of-looting/.
2. https://freebeacon.com/democrats/soros-backed-da-cut-plea-deals
   -with-violent-criminals-represented-by-campaign-donors/.
3. https://virtualglobetrotting.com/map/george-soros-house/view/
   google/.
4. https://thehill.com/homenews/administration/562364-biden-under
   -pressure-to-pick-new-breed-of-federal-prosecutors.
5. Ibid.
6. Ibid.
7. https://nypost.com/2021/06/08/ny-dems-are-proposing-even-more
   -pro-criminal-reforms/.
8. https://ag.ny.gov/press-release/2021/attorney-general-james
   -announces-robust-reforms-police-use-force-laws.
9. https://www.usatoday.com/in-depth/news/investigations/2019/04/24/
   usa-today-revealing-misconduct-records-police-cops/3223984002/.
10. https://thehill.com/homenews/administration/561439-the-memo
    -democrats-face-vulnerability-as-crime-moves-up-voters-agenda.
11. https://www.nytimes.com/2021/06/29/us/politics/jim-clyburn-nina
    -turner-special-election-cleveland.html.

Chapter 18

1. https://www.breitbart.com/politics/2019/10/30/nations-report-card -no-progress-in-either-mathematics-or-reading-performance-in -decade/.
2. https://rethinkingschools.org/articles/activists-mobilize-for-waivers -and-opt-outs-as-biden-mandates-tests/.
3. https://nul.org/sites/default/files/2020-07/Joint%20Civil%20Rts%20 Concerns%20DNC%20Ed%20Platform%20072420%20Final.pdf.
4. https://apnews.com/article/health-oregon-education-coronavirus -pandemic-graduation-1ac30980c9e2d26b288a5341464efde8.
5. https://libertarianhub.com/2021/06/21/vancouver-school-board-is -eliminating-honors-programs-to-achieve-equity/.
6. https://thehayride.com/2021/02/appel-louisiana-joins-oregon-in -dumbing-down-education/.
7. https://www.yahoo.com/now/mcauliffe-says-parents-shouldn-t -173500644.html
8. https://www.dailymail.co.uk/news/article-10062971/Republicans -rage-Biden-weaponizing-DOJ-label-parents-domestic-terrorists .html.
9. Ibid.
10. https://www.foxnews.com/us/minnesota-public-schools-role-play-gay -trans-sex-education.

Conclusion

1. https://www.goodreads.com/quotes/31631-we-are-not-enemies-but -friends-we-must-not-be.
2. 2000 speech to the NAACP.
3. Lincoln's first inaugural address, 1861.

Index